Solzhenitsyn, Tvardovsky, and *Novy Mir*

Solzhenitsyn, Tvardovsky, and *Novy Mir*

Vladimir Lakshin

Translated and edited by Michael Glenny

with additional contributions by
Mary Chaffin and Linda Aldwinckle

The MIT Press
Cambridge, Massachusetts

First MIT Press edition, 1980

The essay "Solzhenitsyn, Tvardovsky, and *Novy Mir*," was originally published in Russian as "Solzhenitsyn, Tvardovsky, y *Novy Mir*" in *The Twentieth Century: A Socio-political Digest and Literary Magazine*, vol. 2 (London: T. C. D. Publications Ltd., 1977). It was also published in French translation as *Réponse à Soljenitsyne* (Paris: Editions Albin Michel, 1977).

This book was set in Fototronic Baskerville by
The Colonial Cooperative Press, Inc.,
and printed and bound by Halliday Lithograph
in the United States of America.

Library of Congress Cataloging in Publication Data

Lakshin, Vladimir Iakovlevich.
  Solzhenitsyn, Tvardovsky and Novy Mir.

  Translation of Solzhenitskiĭ i "Novyĭ mir."
  CONTENTS: Lakshin, V. Solzhenitsyn, Tvardovsky, and Novy Mir.—Chaffin, M. Alexander Tvardovsky—a biographical study. [etc.]
    1. Criticism—Russia—Addresses, essays, lectures.
  2. Tvardovskiĭ, Aleksandr Trifonovich, 1910–1971—Biography—Editing career—Addresses, essays, lectures.
  3. Novyĭ mir—Addresses, essays, lectures.
  4. Solzhenitsyn, Aleksandr Isaevich, 1918– —Criticism and interpretation—Addresses, essays, lectures.
  5. Editor—Russia—Biography—Addresses, essays, lectures. I. Chaffin, Mary. II. Aldwinckle, L.
  III. Title.
PG99.R91 3413, 1980   801'.95'0947   80-21501
ISBN 0-262-12086-0

Contents

Introduction

Michael Glenny

In 1975 there was published in Paris a Russian book, which after some delay has appeared in English, its enigmatic title rendered as *The Oak and the Calf*.* It is Alexander Solzhenitsyn's own story of the mixture of success and failure that met his efforts to have his writing published in the USSR, and in particular of the manoeuvres, stratagems, and political in-fighting leading up to the publication of his first and literally epoch-making work, *One Day in the Life of Ivan Denisovich*. The imagery of the original title—"the calf butted the oak"—infers the notion of a lively, impetuous but inexperienced creature striving in vain to force an immovable object to yield. The "calf" was Solzhenitsyn himself; the "oak" denoted the Soviet Communist Party in its role as guardian of the Marxist-Leninist purity of Soviet literature.

Up to a point the metaphor was a true one: Solzhenitsyn never did achieve publication in his homeland of his major full-length novels—*The First Circle, Cancer Ward*, and *August 1914*—to say nothing of *The Gulag Archipelago*, his terrible indictment of the Soviet system of mass terror and slave labor. To that extent, the calf butted the oak in vain. Yet the suggestion contained in the calf-oak image, that the calf was wholly powerless and ineffectual, is also disingenuous. For the most striking feature of Solzhenitsyn's career is that he—a lone, vulnerable individual—goaded the entire Soviet system into a head-on confrontation, and while in a sense his resulting exile may be said to be a defeat, he not only emerged as the moral victor; he gave the oak a severe battering—and continues to do so. Such, in-

* Alexander Solzhenitsyn, *Bodalsya telyonok s dubom* (literally, *The Calf Butted the Oak*; Paris: YMCA Press, 1975). English-language edition (trans. H. Willetts): *The Oak and the Calf* (New York: Harper & Row; London: Collins-Harvill; 1980). Page references to *The Oak* throughout this book are to this edition.

deed, has been the damage caused to the Soviet regime by *The Gulag Archipelago,* for instance, that "bulldozer" would have been an apter image for the author in relation to the "oak" of the Soviet establishment.

While it implies that Solzhenitsyn's efforts were less effective than they actually were, this discrepancy between image and reality in the book's title (which could be reasonably attributed to artistic license) does not in itself greatly detract from the book's significance; at most it indicates a slightly manipulative choice of wording. "Inside" evidence of the workings of Soviet politics is scarce enough, and *The Oak and the Calf* is important in being one such rare piece of documentation, recounting as it does at first hand a central episode in the history of dissent within the post-Stalin USSR. As such it is to be welcomed, and should be enjoyed by a wide readership as a vivid, interesting, and stylish chapter in the life story of a great writer. When viewing it as potential source material, however, the literary or political historian will be right to approach the book with the caution that is always needed when evaluating an essentially partisan memoir. With the exception of Zhores Medvedev's *Ten Years after Ivan Denisovich** (which, although valuable and informative, cannot qualify as a first-hand source), Solzhenitsyn's report in *The Oak and the Calf* has so far been the only published account of those events by a participant. The articles on Solzhenitsyn that appeared in *Literaturnaya Gazeta* and elsewhere in the Soviet press are mere tactically inspired salvoes of polemical gunfire and of only indirect use as objective evidence. Another man who could have told the story from the vital "third" viewpoint—Alexander Tvar-

* London, 1973.

dovsky, the editor of the journal *Novy Mir,* who published all Solzhenitsyn's work that appeared in the USSR—died in 1971, leaving no known record of Solzhenitsyn's relations with his first (and therefore most important) editor and publisher.

An informed and careful reading of *The Oak and the Calf* will in fact reveal that it is a one-sided account intended to convey a particular view of events. Above all, Solzhenitsyn's treatment in his memoir of Tvardovsky and his colleagues on the *Novy Mir* editorial board (especially his attitude toward Vladimir Lakshin) has caused many readers to be perplexed. Here, it seemed, was Solzhenitsyn presenting himself in a new and, when the implications were considered, distinctly unflattering light. It was surprising enough to read his churlish, dismissive comments on members of the editorial board and discover his apparent scorn for the editorial policies of a magazine that had, after all, propelled him from being an unknown provincial schoolteacher into a literary celebrity of worldwide renown; but most disturbing of all was the carping and unflattering picture that he gave of the two most important figures on the *Novy Mir* board—Tvardovsky, the editor-in-chief, and Lakshin, the leading literary critic—the two men who had done most to advance his literary career and who had strongly, eloquently, and unflinchingly defended Solzhenitsyn when the entire apparatus of the official Soviet politico-literary machine was turned against him. It is this aspect of *The Oak and the Calf* that has raised questions about the author's motivation and the objectivity of his narrative.

Tvardovsky being dead, it seemed for a while doubtful whether anyone else could come forward and speak with sufficient authority to present an alternative insider's account of a story which, in Solzhenitsyn's version, seemed so much at odds with the hitherto accepted view of the harmony and solidarity that had apparently characterized relations between Solzhenitsyn and *Novy Mir*. Who but Solzhenitsyn and Lakshin had supported Tvardovsky's widow at the funeral and had shaken hands at the graveside? Who but Solzhenitsyn had written a moving eulogy on the dead poet-editor?

In fact the riposte to Solzhenitsyn was not slow in coming. Only a few months after its publication, in no more time than it took for a smuggled copy of *The Oak and the Calf* to reach Lakshin in Moscow and for him to read it, he began to write the essay which forms the principal contribution to this collection of studies on the nexus between Solzhenitsyn, Tvardovsky, and the journal *Novy Mir*. Written by the man best fitted to do so—Lakshin was professionally very close to both Tvardovsky and Solzhenitsyn—the essay is an avowed polemic which sets out to put the record straight by challenging and refuting Solzhenitsyn's version of his relations with *Novy Mir* and with Tvardovsky in particular, a version which Lakshin characterizes as unjust, biased, and self-serving.

Since Lakshin is little known outside the USSR, readers may find it helpful to be given a brief sketch of his career and an indication of his position in the world of Russian letters. Vladimir Yakovlevich Lakshin was born in Moscow on 6 May 1933, the son of an actor at the Moscow Arts Theater. Even before graduating from Moscow University in 1955 he had his first article published in *Novy Mir,* and in 1958 became a regular contributor. After some time spent teaching

Russian literature at Moscow University and a two-year stint on the newspaper *Literaturnaya Gazeta,* he was invited by Alexander Tvardovsky in 1962 to join the editorial board of *Novy Mir* and to be its chief literary critic. From then on Lakshin's life was linked with *Novy Mir;* he became a close friend and confidant of Tvardovsky and from 1966 he unofficially carried out the duties of Tvardovsky's deputy. When the editorial board was broken up in January 1970, along with all his colleagues Lakshin lost both his seat on the board and the post of head of literary criticism. At present he works as a consultant to the journal *Inostrannaya Literatura [Foreign Literature].*

Vladimir Lakshin is the author of several books and about a hundred articles on the history of Russian literature, including studies on Herzen, Turgenev, Dostoyevsky, Blok, and the playwright Ostrovsky. Most notably Lakshin has written many articles and two books on Tolstoy and Chekhov. He also played an important role in the publication during the 1960s of the works of Mikhail Bulgakov, several of which had remained unpublished since that author's death in 1940, having been preserved by the efforts of his widow for more than two decades, during which the work of this great and highly original writer was ignored and all but forgotten.

In the 1960s Lakshin also wrote a great deal on current issues in Soviet literature, in particular on the writings of Fyodor Abramov, Georgii Vladimov, Pavel Nilin, Efim Dorosh, I. Grekova, and Vitaly Syomin. But what brought Lakshin really widespread recognition was a cycle of articles devoted to an analysis of the works of Alexander Solzhenitsyn and a series of thematic articles on general literary questions—"Ivan

Denisovich, His Friends and Foes" (*Novy Mir,* 1/1964);
"Writer, Reader, Critic" (4/1965 and 8/1966); "The Sowing and the Harvest" (9/1968); and others. These articles were subjected to the most savage attacks by the "official" hacks of Soviet criticism.

His credo as a literary critic was perhaps best formulated by Lakshin in a broad-ranging review entitled "The Critic Today and Tomorrow," which appeared in the journal *Voprosy Literatury* [*Problems of Literature*], issue of November 1968:

Undoubtedly [Lakshin wrote] the appraisal of a book, an attitude toward it, and a recommendation to readers is an important element of criticism. Even more important, though, are the ideas that it contains. Criticism, however, which assumes the function of the needle on a dial and merely awards grades to the author ("a great success," or "a serious failure") can surely have little more than mechanical significance. It cannot be regarded as a form of creative literature. Of course, even in its restricted function as an indicator, criticism should possess such qualities as objectivity, reasonableness, and tolerance. By the nature of his duties a critic is, as it were, obliged to carry a gun, which he must use with extreme circumspection, not reaching instantly for his holster every time a literary unknown comes into sight. . . .

. . . If the work of a writer is an artistic, organically whole creation, it is not subject to any previous literary "determinants," and it must not be judged by its separate and individual features but in accordance with what is new and unique in its content as a whole. A true, profound critical appraisal, therefore, can only arise from understanding, and understanding comes from analysis of the work. That is why I think an objective, sensitive, and precise analysis of a work is the core of all serious, thorough criticism, and from the character of that analysis one may distinguish the journeyman critic from the master critic.

The journeyman critic is prepared to write on any subject, to assess everything that comes to hand and to take on any literary job; his attitude to the appraisal of a work is that of a professional taster invited to classify the bouquet of a wine or a blend of tea.

Criticism regarded as a vocation, however, is, like literature itself, more selective about the object of its attention. It derives from a lively interest in a particular author, in a particular book that attracts by the enigmatic quality of arousing our love, or, on the other hand, our indignation. The richer the critic's intellectual world, the broader is the range of his likes and dislikes, and the more naturally does a general view of the literary world come to life under his pen. But behind all genuinely influential criticism there inevitably lies a powerful inner impulse: 'I must talk about this book; I want to describe how I understood it, what I thought about it and about the life which it depicts.' This impulse is essential to the critic himself, and is therefore, perhaps equally essential for the reader. . . .

In the final analysis, we should make the same demands of a critical article as we do of any other kind of literary work: richness of content, sincerity, and mastery of form. And to this I would add one more: the topicality and timeliness of what the critic has to say.

Real criticism—criticism which deals with ideas—must inevitably be concerned with the same anxieties and problems that consciously or unconsciously preoccupy the majority of its contemporaries. The artist or poet may comfort himself with the thought that even if he is not fully understood now, he will be understood and appreciated later (although this attitude does smack a little of self-deception). The critic is completely deprived of this hope. He is wholly in the contemporary world, in the here and now of literature, and if his voice does not ring out at full strength for a contemporary readership, then it will probably never be audible at all. That is one reason, incidentally, why it is impossible to imagine a critical article being written "for the desk drawer."

Vladimir Lakshin himself is precisely such a master critic, a critic by vocation, whose articles, essays, and books are distinguished by their vigor and trenchancy, their mastery of form—and by their topicality and timeliness. The essay which follows, having first circulated in Russia in typescript form by the process known as *samizdat,* was written for the hundreds of thousands who made up the loyal and admiring readership of *Novy Mir* during the period of Tvardovsky's editorship. Solzhenitsyn's book *The Oak and the Calf,* of which almost half is devoted to the same theme, has been translated into many languages and published in hundreds of thousands of copies. As has been suggested, there are features of this book which may cause the reader to wonder whether Solzhenitsyn's view of *Novy Mir* and Tvardovsky is entirely trustworthy and credible. Lakshin now tells us the same story but from a different viewpoint. A distinguished critic and literary historian, Lakshin in his essay depicts many of the unsuspected complexities and clashes at the center of Russian literature and literary politics during that crucial decade between 1961 and 1971. At the same time it is a tense, dramatic account of the relationship between two figures who have become legendary. Solzhenitsyn has given us his version. Tvardovsky is dead and can no longer speak for himself. Anyone reading Lakshin's controversial essay, however, cannot fail to be aware that Tvardovsky lives on in the hearts of his friends and that they are well able to speak out on his behalf. In addition to Lakshin's essay, two writers specializing in modern Soviet literature have each made a contribution to this collection. Mary Chaffin has given us a biographical study of Alexander Tvardovsky, and Linda Aldwinckle has analyzed the literary politics of *Novy Mir* during Tvardovsky's editorship; their scholarly treatment of these topics is intended to provide an informed, objective background to the Lakshin-Solzhenitsyn controversy.

Alexander Tvardovsky and Vladimir Lakshin, 1965

Solzhenitsyn, Tvardovsky, and *Novy Mir*

Vladimir Lakshin

Translated from the Russian by Michael Glenny

I was prompted to write this essay by Alexander Solzhenitsyn's book *The Oak and the Calf,* published in Paris in 1975. It cost me much long and hard thought before deciding to record for the friends of *Novy Mir—*the journal in which Solzhenitsyn's *One Day in the Life of Ivan Denisovich* was first published—the thoughts and recollections evoked in me by *The Oak and the Calf,* and my present attitude toward its author. I would ask those who may happen to read this to forgive a certain untidiness in its construction, some repetition, and in particular its over personal tone; I am not writing a newspaper article, but am attempting to come to terms with a part of my own life.

For more than ten years my personal and professional life was bound up with A. T. Tvardovsky's journal *Novy Mir,* and with Solzhenitsyn too, who entered Russian literature through its doors.

From the first moment—it was in early December 1961—that I began to read, in confidence and with every possible warning, the manuscript of *Ivan Denisovich* which Tvardovsky had passed on to me (as yet untitled, but headed with the mysterious sign "Shch—854"), I was fired by the calm truthfulness of this work, thrilled by the author's fearless audacity and high purpose; his narrative of prison-camp life was all the more convincing for being written, as it were, from below, from the viewpoint of a peasant, and for the imperturbable calm with which it described a *happy* day. And then there was the astounding skill in depicting, so economically yet so vividly, a large number of characters and their lives—just as though you, the reader, were living among them. The style, too, was novel and original. There was no question about it: I realized this author's outstanding talent at once, wholly and unconditionally, and I liked Alexander Tvardovsky all the more for having so enthusiastically and courageously perceived the artistic truth of this story.

During the following weeks and months, whenever we met in our friendly circle, we talked of nothing else but how to publish it. We devised the most fantastic plans, discussed what line of approach to take and what would be the most sensible way of going about it. It now seems, with hindsight, that what we did was all so simple, that it was the only possible way: to send the manuscript to Khrushchev, arouse his enthusiasm, and get permission "from the top." . . .

It is a childish error to overestimate Tvardovsky's influence "at the top." Many people thought that he even had access to Stalin, but in fact he never once met Stalin or spoke to him. And as for his relations with Khrushchev, it was assumed that they were so friendly that Tvardovsky could simply drop in on Khrushchev for tea. In one of his poems Tvardovsky ridiculed the simple-minded reader who was convinced that it was no trouble at all for the poet "to raise a little question of mine" in between discussing other matters with Khrushchev (Tvardovsky's mailbag contained a considerable number of such requests).

In this case, though, the "question" was a special one, and the editor of *Novy Mir* knew that only too well. In the spring of 1962 Yury Bondaryov's *Silence* had only just squeaked through into print, after a brush with the censor; it had contained only one powerful scene—the father's arrest—which dealt with forbidden subject matter. And here was a Soviet prison camp, described so fully and with such truth—could there be any comparison? In the handbook of the censor (Glavlit)* the subject of "places of detention" was given special emphasis as being a state secret. Publication of Solzhenitsyn's story would have violated that prohibition, but it might also, if it succeeded in being published, open the way into literature for the whole prison-camp theme. In this instance a literary question coincided with a most crucial political issue. A secret, behind-the-scenes struggle was in progress over the whole question of the prison camps and the rehabilitation of their victims; Khrushchev himself would alternately advance and retreat in his disclosures about Stalin and one careless, false step might ruin everything.

In the summer and autumn of 1962, as a newly appointed member of *Novy Mir*'s editorial board, I took part in the preliminary discussion of Solzhenitsyn's story and its preparation for publication. I remember how concerned Tvardovsky was that there should be absolute unanimity among the members of the editorial board in this matter, and I, among his other editorial colleagues, did my best to fortify his resolution once he had taken this courageous decision. Naturally we are all only human, and the degree of doubt and hesitation differed among the various members of the board, but on the essential point—that the story *must be published*—the board was unanimous. In June 1962, before any approaches were made to higher authority, we actually took a formal vote on it: everyone raised a hand to vote in favor.

From then on, step by step, the story of Solzheni-

* *Glavlit* is the Russian acronym for the body which censors all printed matter in the USSR. Each *Glavlit* censor is supplied with a secret book of instructions, constantly amended and updated, which lists the topics that may not be mentioned in print.

tsyn's connection with *Novy Mir* became a part of my own personal destiny. Together with A. Tvardovsky and A. G. Dement'ev I took part in drafting and editing Tvardovsky's letter to Khrushchev about *Ivan Denisovich*. As is now common knowledge, the decision to publish it was taken by the Presidium of the Central Committee of the Communist Party of the Soviet Union after twice debating the question. It was no secret that the story was published "with the knowledge and approval of the Central Committee," as they said in those days, yet it very soon became evident that the story had some fairly influential enemies.

After some extravagant praise (V. Ermilov wrote in *Pravda* that it was a work "of Tolstoyan power"), there was a gradual switch to hostile abuse of Solzhenitsyn in the press and at writers' meetings, at first in fairly restrained and oblique manner, but then month by month the attacks grew fiercer and more malicious. In the summer of 1963 I wrote an article, which was published in the January 1964 issue of *Novy Mir*, entitled "Ivan Denisovich, His Friends and Foes." The article was correctly interpreted by both the friends and foes of *Novy Mir*. The journal was subjected to a hail of libelous comment, refutations, and editorials (in *Literaturnaya Gazeta*, *Literaturnaya Rossiya*, *Moskva*, *Ogonyok*, and other periodicals), in which Solzhenitsyn's story, described as truthful and in general written "from a party standpoint" was contrasted with my article, which was alleged to have distorted it.

Solzhenitsyn does not care to recall this, or rather he recalls it as follows: he describes how they began to publish, ". . . a second and a third assailant, tearing the short stories to pieces first, then the tale that had won favor with the All Highest [*Ivan Denisovich*]—and still no one intervened" (p. 65). This is untrue. *Novy*

Mir spoke out in its defense. Among my papers I still have a letter from Solzhenitsyn dated 4 February 1964, in which he warmly thanked the journal and myself for my article defending him against the absurd attacks; furthermore, the article it seems, had even been something of a revelation to Solzhenitsyn himself: "An article like that gives one a sense of having actually grown wiser." Generous and, perhaps, exaggerated praise, which in those days came quite naturally to him.

I greeted Solzhenitsyn's novels *The First Circle* and *Cancer Ward* as a literary triumph and with personal delight, regarding them as a confirmation of the enormous power and vitality of his creative gift. They did not, perhaps, have quite the absolute perfection and artistic richness of *Ivan Denisovich,* not all the scenes and characters were faultless, but this was redeemed by their broadness of aim, the diversity of fresh ideas and images which they contained, and their revitalization of the novel form. It meant that the novella was not just a chance success, not just a flash in the pan, and that at last we had a writer who called to mind the giants of Russian literature of the past. The journal was unable to publish the novels for reasons which were, as the saying goes, "beyond editorial control." But for a long time we hoped that by some miracle we might be able to publish them; we made repeated attempts to do so and, to support the author, we signed contracts with him for these works on the most generous terms.

In January 1966, at the very time when, alarmed by the seizure of his manuscripts in Teush's apartment, Solzhenitsyn, as he says in his book, "Almost every night . . . fully expected to be arrested" (p. 104)

Novy Mir published his short story "Zakhar-the-Pouch." Not everyone on the editorial board liked this story, but they all agreed that we had to support the author in his difficult situation by publishing it. And in August 1966, when for a long time not a single newspaper or journal in the USSR had had a kind word to say about Solzhenitsyn, I managed to publish in *Novy Mir* an extensive, sympathetic analysis of his short story "Matryona's House," in which the unintelligent strictures of the official critics were contrasted with the opinions expressed by our readers. On 5 October 1966 Solzhenitsyn sent me, by the way, a long and grateful letter, in which he made the most flattering comments on my "excellent critical style" and even listed its particular features point by point. It is perhaps immodest of me to recall this—but what is one to do when in his book Solzhenitsyn describes the vicious attack on "Matryona's House" that appeared in *Izvestiya*, yet writes not a word about *Novy Mir*'s defense of this story? In other instances, too, Solzhenitsyn's memory is equally selective.

I am writing all this now to show how dear Solzhenitsyn was to me, both personally and as a literary figure. As for myself, I will always be proud of having assisted at the emergence of this remarkable new talent, and of having helped Tvardovsky to support and defend him in those early days when his voice, sharp and unfamiliar, was first heard in literature.

During my years at *Novy Mir* I came to regard Solzhenitsyn as a person close to me, and I never doubted his kind feelings toward me. But then in 1970, no more than two months after the enforced break-up of the journal, a quarrel broke out between us by letter which led to an unspoken, undeclared estrangement. Unexpectedly for Tvardovsky and myself, Solzhenitsyn, on the flimsiest of pretexts, committed to paper his detailed, though belated accusations against the journal's editorship. The content of these letters is very accurately reproduced on pp. 281–285 of *The Oak and the Calf.* With hindsight, he blamed the journal for the colorlessness of its last issues, and claimed that in the 1960s *Novy Mir* had suffered a defeat "in its rivalry" (?) with *samizdat;* with particular virulence he condemned the dismissed members of the editorial board for not having put up a "courageous resistance" when they were relieved of their duties, and so on.

In *The Oak and the Calf,* Solzhenitsyn writes: "I did not conceal from the dismissed editors my disapproval of their whole policy at the time of crisis and final collapse. [(What a choice of words! To say this about the officially imposed dissolution of the editorial board!— V.L.)] The same message was conveyed to Tvardovsky, though without the detailed reasons given here" (p. 284). Solzhenitsyn is mistaken. He asked that Tvardovsky should be informed of the content of his letters to me, and I gave copies of them to Tvardovsky. The latter was indignant, and with his typical abrupt directness he wanted to reply to Solzhenitsyn. I persuaded him not to, saying that I would answer him myself. Otherwise it would have become *their* quarrel, and given the intemperance of both their characters, the dispute would only have brought joy to their ill-wishers ("Look," they would have said, "no sooner is the *Novy Mir* team broken up than Tvardovsky and Solzhenitsyn are at each other's throats!")

Tvardovsky agreed. . . . In the letters I wrote in reply, which Solzhenitsyn does not mention in *The Oak,* but of which Tvardovsky was fully informed, I wrote, *inter alia,* as follows:

I fully sympathize with your wish that "as we move into the seventies, a spade should be called a spade." But you are making a mistake if you think that anything you say is, as it were, a pronouncement made by history itself. I am not convinced that history will agree with everything you say. Unfortunately you almost always harbor the most childish illusions, you easily get events out of their true perspective, and you obviously yield to the moods and impressions of a narrow, cliquish, sectarian prejudice. And there is so much naive improvisation in your historical prognoses and assessments. [. . .] I realize, of course, that you are biased, and that these assessments are in large measure the result of the unwholesome circumstances and unnatural situation in which you, as a writer, have been placed. But while remaining an unswerving admirer of your literary talent, I sincerely regret that your sociopolitical views should be expressed in terms of such falsity. (8th May 1970)

People who were close to Solzhenitsyn at the time informed me that he did not want to publicize our correspondence—and so it disappeared below the surface, to reappear only now in the pages of *The Oak*.

My last meeting with Solzhenitsyn took place in December 1971, and although it was not particularly cordial, it was at least decently polite; it took place at Tvardovsky's funeral, and we shook each other firmly by the hand at the graveside. I had the impression that Solzhenitsyn had by then gained a new understanding of Tvardovsky and of *Novy Mir,* and his obituary of Tvardovsky seemed to confirm this. Afterward (to complete the picture of our relationship before the publication of *The Oak*) he sent me a handwritten invitation to attend the Nobel prizegiving ceremony in his apartment, which I did not decline. The ceremony, as we know, never took place.

When Solzhenitsyn was expelled from the country, I

naturally rejected the insistent requests for a "comment" or an interview, which were intended as part of the chorus of officially inspired abuse which followed him into exile. And although I disagreed with many of the speeches and statements which he had made since 1970; although, with the exception of a few brilliant chapters, I did not like *August 1914*; and although his article about repentance in the symposium *From Under the Rubble** struck me as perplexing and somewhat ridiculous, I did not feel able to write anything against him either for publication or in *samizdat*.

"Whenever my friends say stupid things, I try to look at them in profile," a famous Frenchman once said. I thought Solzhenitsyn would come to his senses; I believed that what he had said as a writer in his best books, written in his homeland, was much more important for all of us, both for our country and for men of goodwill all over the world, than his ill-considered interviews and improvised tirades on some burning political topic of the moment. I was also restrained by the consideration that no matter how bizarre his political theories and his off-the-cuff remarks might be, it was wrong to obstruct that movement of healthy, cleansing criticism [of the Soviet system] which was linked with the name of the author of *Ivan Denisovich*. Yet it seemed that he himself was obstructing it so badly that no one was in a position to help him. Would it not therefore be better to speak out frankly and without restraint?

In *The Oak and the Calf* he has insulted the memory of a man who was very dear to me, whom I regarded as a second father, and he has offended many of my friends and colleagues. But chiefly he has poured arro-

---

* Agursky et al., *Iz-pod glyb: sbornik statei* (Paris, 1974).

gant scorn on the journal which was the very cradle of his own literary career, and he has besmirched the *cause* of that journal, which in the eyes of millions of people in our country and abroad was a worthwhile and honorable cause.

The challenge has been made, and I will pick up the gauntlet. Fortunately, Solzhenitsyn is no longer in any personal danger. The halo of world fame has meant that the long-awaited financial and physical security are now his. Tvardovsky is in the grave, and I feel it my duty to reply on his behalf. Knowing the conditions under which we live [in the Soviet Union], Solzhenitsyn may have hoped that I and others who are not subservient hacks toeing the Party line would feel obliged to remain silent and swallow his memoirs without protest. In this he is mistaken.

I shall not mention anything here which I cannot personally vouch for—such as the circumstances of Solzhenitsyn's life outside the confines of *Novy Mir,* or his activities after 1970. But speaking as one of the personages in his latest book, there are one or two things that I *do* know and *can* vouch for.

So let there be an end to restraint: The time has come to settle accounts and say farewell—to say farewell on this earth forever, or at all events until in some future age, under another sky and on another shore, someone whose justice is beyond question may be the arbiter of our dispute.

The author of *The Oak* reproaches us Russians with being excessively cautious, sluggish, and lazy. True, we are. He, by contrast, is always in a hurry and is now hurrying without any need. He is hastening to publish in various [Western] journals extracts and chapters from previously published works which were excluded from the earlier text, and which on examination have invariably proved to be inferior, smacking as they do of over-acidulous journalese; he is also busily collecting and publishing autobiographical material.

All this is very unlike the behavior of writers of the last century, who kept their diaries, notes, letters, drafts, and variants well out of the public eye, sometimes even posthumously placing a ban on their publication for thirty, fifty, or a hundred years out of an understandable modesty or consideration for the feelings of those still alive. In more recent years Thomas Mann placed just such a ban on his correspondence, and Hemingway laid a posthumous veto on the greater part of his archive.

Solzhehitsyn, however, does not trust history (or at least literary history) to arrive at a correct assessment of anything concerning his life story, and he hastens to pronounce his judgment on everything—a judgment that is final and without appeal. (True, it is only final for today; tomorrow his judgment on the same people and events will be different, but the infallible judge does not even entertain this likelihood.) Least of all does Solzhenitsyn trust his potential biographers, and he hastens to issue an authorized version of his career as a writer, together with the whole of the literary world immediately surrounding him.

Solzhenitsyn describes the genre of *The Oak and the Calf* as "sketches of literary life." This is obviously a misapprehension. The book contains nothing about literature except the works of Solzhenitsyn himself, and nothing about life except that which is immediately linked with his own. As if in passing, listed together in parentheses, like a perfunctory list in a newspaper report, he mentions Shukshin, Mozhaev,

Tendryakov, Belov, and Soloukhin—with never a word about their works.

And indeed, what kind of literary life can there have been before him or in his time if Solzhenitsyn is accustomed to prejudge it in these terms: "The new works being printed, which till then [1961] had merely amused me, now began to irritate me" (p. 12)? In fact, as a rule Solzhenitsyn did not read the works of Soviet writers, because "I knew in advance that there was nothing worthwhile in any of them." True, the author of *The Oak* says that during the 1960s he somewhat modified this pessimistic view. But—he has seldom praised a single book or spoken with genuine sympathy about any writer except himself.

It would seem that Mikhail Bulgakov is a figure of incontestable significance, yet even about Bulgakov Solzhenitsyn says: "The perverse obsession with the forces of evil (and this is not the first book in which it appears: it is there ad nauseam in his *Diavoliada* collection). . . . And how do we explain the extraordinary interpretation of the gospel story, presented so as to degrade Christ, as though it were all seen through the eyes of Satan . . . ?" (p. 238). Thus writes Solzhenitsyn about the novel *The Master and Margarita,* in connection with my article about it, in which he also found nothing but "a farrago of evasions."

He comments on no other novelists at all, and his remarks on Bulgakov contain a strong dose of writer's jealousy.

I remember a conversation in a car, when we were driving out to Tvardovsky's *dacha* (this episode is described in *The Oak*). Solzhenitsyn cautiously chided me for spending all my time writing about Bulgakov, although the fame of *The Master and Margarita* was already on the decline: soon, he said the world's attention would be taken up by other names, other works. "Which?" I inquired, not knowing what he meant. To my simple-minded question he gave only a vague, evasive reply. Now I understand rather better the meaning of our conversation in the car . . . .

In other words, to call this book "Sketches of Literary Life" is really an inept exaggeration. Rather they are memoirs: a book about himself, and about a few people connected with a certain stage in his career.

The public is always fascinated by the life of a great artist who has acquired renown through his works. As a supplement to his written work, by merely living his life a famous writer is, as it were, writing yet another book for the benefit of posterity—even if he never leaves an autobiography such as Herzen's *My Past and Thoughts* or Goethe's *Dichtung und Wahrheit*. The life of a Pushkin or a Balzac is, so to speak, a well-known novel. By fragments the biographers and memoirists recreate a picture of the artist's life. But in the minds of his readers there is preserved and consolidated a *legend* created by his life, and it is that which sets the seal on our perception of that writer's books.

Solzhenitsyn is unwilling to entrust the telling of his life story to anyone else; he has decided that he himself will bequeath his self-portrait to posterity and record his own lineaments in a literary mirror. According to his conception, this should be a full-length portrait of a hero of the age, depicted among a host of callow striplings and literary pygmies—an aim reminiscent of the obligation to create a "positive hero" in a work of socialist realism.

No doubt an eye less biased than mine will find that this book also has its virtues. And even I am not blind to what is good in it. It has truthful things to say and there are some powerful passages in it, especially those which give us insights into the author's own inner nature and where he manages to avoid excessive self-satisfaction. But I am not writing a review. It has fallen to my lot to be a witness in a trial which the author has instigated, and I must give my testimony.

For *The Oak* is neither memoir nor history. It is not history, because Solzhenitsyn prefers not to mention a great many things that did occur and describes many others—intentionally or accidentally—in terms that differ from what really happened. Nor is it a memoir in the usual sense, because the book contains many personages with features that have been strikingly added or altered by the author's imagination, yet which, as in lampoons, bear the names of real people.

How was it that he felt no twinge of conscience when he wrote, and then published in twelve languages, his belated pamphlet against *Novy Mir,* against people, of whom one is in the grave and the others are not in exactly the most favorable position to polemicize with him?

But perhaps it would, after all, be better to pass by this book in dignified silence, as though ignoring it? It is always both tedious and unpleasant to have to explain and justify oneself in the face of libel. It is infinitely less disturbing to console oneself with the high-minded conviction that "history will judge," "mud doesn't stick to a good name," and, in general terms, *qui s'excuse, s'accuse.*

Alas, history is a capricious lady; she too has her favorites and her tattle-tales, and at times she lends her authority too trustingly to judgments and character evaluations that are suggested by her favorites. She too must be made, at times, to explain and prove: "If the child doesn't cry, the mother won't know whether anything is wrong."

The great poet and journal editor N.A. Nekrasov,* who is often cited as a precursor of Tvardovsky, was persecuted all his life by the unscrupulous calumnies which denigrated him as a poet and as a man, but he made a rule for himself: he would never reply to slander, never attempt to refute anyone, never enter into a dispute. He was at the point of intersection of many complex human and social cross-currents and was in consequence subject to every conceivable form of libelous attack. Accused of dishonesty in the matter of the "Ogaryov inheritance," he was branded as grasping and acquisitive. He was scolded for his dubious acquaintances, for playing cards with the censor, and for insincerity in his views. Two of his closest colleagues on the *Sovremennik*, M. Antonovich and Y. Zhukovsky, wrote a scurrilous pamphlet entitled *Materials for a Descriptive Study of Russian Literature (1868)*, which hinted that as a journalist Nekrasov was guilty of treachery and dishonest intentions. People muttered about him, spread malicious innuendoes, gossiped—and Nekrasov remained silent. His silence was either due to the perplexity of a sensitive, conscientious man who, for all the falsity of the slander aimed at him, felt that there was nevertheless always something with which to reproach himself, or it was motivated by a proud hope that he would be exonerated by history. In this he was

* Nikolai Nekrasov (1821–78). A popular poet, whose verse had a strong revolutionary tinge, Nekrasov exposed the injustices and hardships of the Russian peasant's life. He was also editor of two of the most widely-read, liberal and progressive literary journals of his time: *Sovremennik (The Contemporary)* from 1847 to 1866, and *Otechestvennyie zapiski (Notes of the Fatherland)* from 1868 to 1877 (Editor's note).

wrong. For a hundred years his good name was dogged
by those age-old libels and accusations. Only in the
last few years have diligent literary historians begun to
unravel that tangled skein, and it now turns out that
neither in the Ogaryov case nor in the conflict with his
colleagues at the *Sovremennik* were there the slightest
grounds for Nekrasov to reproach himself—he had simply preferred not to have to justify himself.

Nowadays, thanks to the power of the mass media,
every rumor and prejudiced judgment, especially with
the added authority of a famous name, can be incredi-
bly contagious and liable to spread like an epidemic.
That is why it is no longer possible to allow oneself the
luxury of silence and of treating the written word with
proud disdain.

I shall therefore set about, without squeamishness,
to analyze the accusations and reproaches made in the
Oak and the Calf against the *Novy Mir* of the 1960s and
its editor, Tvardovsky.

Several people who have read this book have expressed the opinion that despite the slurs cast upon
him by Solzhenitsyn, Tvardovsky emerges from it as a
strong and attractive figure. I am glad if this is so, if
the personality has managed to overcome the author's
tendentiousness. But I cannot reconcile myself to this
depiction of Alexander Tvardovsky. To do so is perhaps easier for someone who did not know Tvardovsky, or knew him only slightly. For those, however,
who knew him well and intimately, who lived through
those years by his side, this picture is an insult to his
memory.

Here, for example is how Solzhenitsyn, without a
trace of embarrassment on his features, accuses Tvardovsky of delay over *Ivan Denisovich:* ". . . how can I

refrain from saying now that Tvardovsky 'let slip a golden opportunity, missed the flood-tide . . ." (p. 32). Solzhenitsyn is under the impression that Khrushchev was simply waiting to read his novella, and that Tvardovsky bungled his job as a link in the chain of transmission by delaying it for several months.

I have already mentioned above the extent to which anyone aware of the true circumstances is flabbergasted by such an attitude. But the most amazing thing of all is that it is actually refuted in this very book by the author himself. Solzhenitsyn recalls how, at their first meeting, Tvardovsky asked Solzhenitsyn not to hasten him with *Ivan Denisovich*, and that the journal would supply all the necessary pressure. "I wasn't intending to; I had been spared the Lubyanka, and asked no more"—comments the author (pp. 31–32). Again, on the discussion of the story, he has this to say: "Had I gone mad? Surely the editorial board could not seriously believe the thing was publishable?" (p. 24). That was what Solzhenitsyn thought *then*—and it is the truth. Now he accuses us of dragging our feet. How many more of such contradictions and hasty, rash statements are there in his book— you can scoop them up in handfuls!

The author of *The Oak* now grumbles that Tvardovsky ". . . spent a long time trying to write a fitting preface to the story (though strictly speaking there was no need for it: why make excuses?)" (p. 33). My God, the things that Solzhenitsyn has forgotten or has chosen not to remember! The editor-in-chief might indeed have played for safety—he could have simply published the novella and refrained from pronouncing a direct opinion on it. But for Tvardovsky the publication of *Ivan Denisovich* was a decisive personal *act*. K. Fedin and A. Surkov, from whom among others he

sought advice in an attempt to win support, told him
that the cause was hopeless and that he had no business trying to push such a manuscript under the noses
of the "top brass." Tvardovsky, however, not only did
just that, but in his editor's preface announced to the
whole world that he personally assumed responsibility
[for publication], that Solzhenitsyn's story was not being published by an oversight but as a conscious, force-
ful step—and thereby put all the strength of his authority into defending the novice writer from his
influential enemies. And for the reader, too, a recommendation from the poet who created *Vasily Tyorkin,*
and who did not squander his praise, was of no little
significance. But what is all that to Solzhenitsyn today? As the proverb says: "Give him an inch and he
takes a mile."

I remember how in 1969 we were talking about one
of Solzhenitsyn's outbursts, and Tvardovsky recited
expressively a few lines of verse that Marshak had
translated into Russian:

A sparrow fed a cuckoo,
A homeless ball of feathers;
What did that cuckoo do?
Killed his adoptive father. . . .

And he laughed mirthlessly.

Solzhenitsyn seldom uttered any of those well-de-
served kind words that he might have said about Tvardovsky, apparently never saw his many remarkable
characteristics. One can, I suppose, hardly reproach
him for that—if there is no crime, there can be no trial.
Nor does he like Tvardovsky's poetry, with the possible
exception of *Vasily Tyorkin;* that, too, is his affair. But
the fact that he has exaggerated, invented, and blown

up Tvardovsky's weaknesses out of all proportion—that is unforgivable.

Three fatal shortcomings of Tvardovsky are cited as casting a deep shadow on his majestic figure:

Cowardice in the face of insignificant people and dangerous situations; cowardice, linked with the fact that Tvardovsky carried "a little red booklet" in his breast pocket. ". . . Tvardovsky was doomed to despair and to seek oblivion in drink whenever he received an unfriendly telephone call from some minor official in the Central Committee, and to blossom whenever the head of the 'Cultural Department' bestowed a crooked smile upon him" (p. 67).

Drunkenness, which Solzhenitsyn perceives as cowardice, drunkenness which weakened Tvardovsky and bordered on a breakdown of personality. "Perhaps out of consideration for Tvardovsky it would have been better not to bring all these details under the spotlight. But if I didn't, the reader would not understand how unsteady, and how helplessly limp at times were the hands that managed *Novy Mir* . . ." (p. 78).

Pride, which made him, even in the editorial board and with his close colleagues, structure all relationships on a Stalinist model. Tvardovsky, says Solzhenitsyn, "was incapable of close association with his peers" (p. 49). ". . . The liberal journal was settling into a hierarchical and conservative mold. Only favorable and fulsome reports were sent 'upward' . . ." (p. 57).

I declare that everything said about Tvardovsky in this vein is either a blatant *untruth*, rooted in Solzhenitsyn's hopelessly obtuse incomprehension of Tvardovsky's nature and character, or is that nasty, slimy, slanderous kind of *half-truth* that is worse than a conscious lie.

It is a fact that Tvardovsky traveled a long, circuitous path of inward progress and development to reach the convictions that he held as editor of *Novy Mir* in the 1960s, the period in which the journal achieved worldwide fame. His mind was not programmed in advance. Despite the apparent conservatism of his tastes, he was in the highest degree capable of welcoming any changes for the better and of assimilating what was new. In 1960 his attitude to many things differed from the views he had held in 1950, and in 1970 he thought otherwise than in 1960, and his death cut short this developing process. His usual reaction to a book, a person, or an event which surprised him was: "I've only now realized . . ." Should one see this as a weakness in him, as inadequacy? No. To me this shows a lively strength of mind and moral courage. He might well have repeated Pushkin's words: "To make mistakes and to revise one's judgments is inherent in any thinking creature. To make a frank admission of this requires spiritual strength."

In fact, Tvardovsky did not regard his Party membership card as a meaningless scrap of cardboard. It was linked in his mind with a very genuine, honest—perhaps even hypertrophied—sense of duty. But that was not all. Even though, with the passage of time, his sharp, critical mind had already stripped away and discarded a great many of the prescriptions and rules of a false dogmatism, the actual idea of communism as of a happy state of democratic equality still ruled his mind and was an essential part of his personal ideal. Into that ideal he also incorporated everything that was best in the social and moral experience of mankind—and only in the consciousness of that ideal was he able to live and write with a sense of purpose.

In his fanatical intolerance Solzhenitsyn sees the matter quite simply: as far as he is concerned "the little red booklet" means the destruction of a human being, the mark of Cain—in the same degree, obviously, that he regards a cross worn around the neck as a guarantee of enlightenment and salvation. But is this the real dividing line which separates people into bad and good, noble and villainous, selfish and self-sacrificing, cowardly and courageous? One man believes in the church and in God, another in socialism and in man. Yet either faith can be bigoted, obscurantist and inhumane—or sublime, good, sincere. "You know, there are non-party people who are worse than we Party members . . ."—Tvardovsky used to say, laughingly, about people like Leonid Sobolev and his ilk.* Our world has shown by countless examples that a person may profess any doctrine, may be a member of this or that church, but that when really put to the test his or her true character owes infinitely more to human qualities and attitude to others than to formal belief. Good people, whether believers or unbelievers, understand each other; the religious fanatic or the fanatical atheist—never. But that is by the way.

Naturally Tvardovsky had his illusions, his weaknesses, and his misconceptions, and the journal shared them with its editor-in-chief. Of myself I may say that I would be far from happy to see every single page of my articles of those days reprinted now: they contain words and expressions that were written under constraint, prompted by "tactical considerations" on behalf of the journal; they contain judgments that are

* Leonid Sobolev (1898–1971), after serving in both the Czarist and Soviet navies, became a popular writer of fiction on naval life. A hard-line Stalinist, he was chairman of the Board of Management of the Writers' Union of the RSFSR from 1958 to 1970 (editor's note).

nowadays obviously naive, even ridiculous, in their limited comprehension. "But somehow one doesn't feel ashamed of them, one doesn't feel ashamed at all," as Tvardovsky used to say in such instances. Why not? Simply because there was nothing mean or petty in *Novy Mir.*

What is more, there was never any cowardice in Tvardovsky, and never, above all, in connection with his Party membership or his political standing.

The straightforward, independent, and firm tone in which Tvardovsky used to talk to the most highly-placed people was something worth hearing. Suffice it to recall the occasion in 1961, when with many other writers present, in the Secretariat of the Central Committee he replied to the then powerful L. F. Ilyichov's* remark that Tvardovsky in his speech had not been entirely sincere: "I allow no one, not even the secretary of the Central Committee, to be the judge of my sincerity." Ilyichov gulped with amazement and his face went pale—after which he harbored an increased degree of both dislike and respect for Tvardovsky. One day in my presence Tvardovsky spoke on the editor's telephone with the very highest Party bosses— Brezhnev, Suslov, Ilyichov, and Demichev—and one could not help being astonished at his ability to carry on a conversation with such directness, independence, and dignity, in a manner which impressed anyone of intelligence and reduced arrogant fools to embarrassed silence. "Since you find difficulty in replying, don't

* Leonid Fyodorovich Ilyichov (b. 1906). Career official of the Communist Party of the Soviet Union: 1961, secretary of the Central Committee of the Communist Party of the Soviet Union for cultural affairs; 1968, elected member, USSR Academy of Sciences; 1964, demoted from Central Committee post on Khrushchev's fall; 1965, Deputy Minister of Foreign Affairs; latterly chief Soviet negotiator in border dispute with China.

bother," he said coldly on another occasion, cutting off the mendacious excuses of P. Satyukov, editor-in-chief of *Pravda,* for refusing publication of some of Tvardovsky's poetry. No one ever dared to raise his voice to Tvardovsky, for everyone sensed in him a particular dignity and moral strength, and on more than one occasion I was able to observe how second-grade rapporteurs and important chiefs alike tried to ingratiate themselves with him. He had, of course, a winning charm that derived from simplicity and a gentle sense of humor, but at the same time he also possessed a natural dignity which helped him to maintain a proper distance. Yet he was very far from being naive, and when it was a question of serving the best interests of literature and the good name of *Novy Mir,* he could occasionally be cunning, flexible, and devious—but never at the cost of his personal dignity. In the early part of his book (p. 49) even Solzhenitsyn notes Tvardovsky's ". . . peculiar natural dignity with which he met his enemies (sometimes persons in high places) . . . ," but he soon forgets that and persists, instead, in fashioning a totally different image.

I do not mean that Tvardovsky never experienced fear: in greater or less degree we are all subject to it. Unlike many other people, however, he was able to overcome it, and for that reason he was never a coward. Solzhenitsyn gives a ridiculous description of the fright which, according to him, seized Tvardovsky in Ryazan' while Solzhenitsyn was reading him the manuscript of *The First Circle.* Knowing Tvardovsky, I strongly doubt Solzhenitsyn's version of the scene. Solzhenitsyn is wrong in interpreting Tvardovsky's rambling, late-night remarks in that way. But in order to emphasize Tvardovsky's alleged cowardice, the author of *The Oak* waxes indignant over the fact that Tvardovsky would not take the manuscript of *The First Circle* for safekeeping in the editorial office when he brought it to Tvardovsky for the second time, after the KGB had already seized a copy of the novel. "But if Benckendorff had been stalking a novel, and someone had brought it to Pushkin for safekeeping, we can be sure that he would have eagerly seized the folder, instead of murmuring evasively. . . . The poet's standing in the nation has changed, and so have the poets themselves," moralizes Solzhenitsyn (p. 108).

Let us leave aside the false pathos. The great Pushkin, alas, was no model of civil courage, and if Solzhenitsyn had a better knowledge of Russian literary history he would never have attempted to draw such a parallel. Let us instead turn our attention to something else. In 1965, before the misfortune occurred, Tvardovsky was offended by the lack of confidence shown by Solzhenitsyn in his insistence in taking the manuscript of *The First Circle* out of the safe, despite heated attempts to persuade him to leave it there. Within the premises of *Novy Mir* no one would have dared to confiscate it without Tvardovsky's consent. "That will never happen as long as I am editor," said Tvardovsky firmly, banging his palm on the table. But after Solzhenitsyn, pursuing his own devious paths, had managed to be too clever by half and the manuscript of the novel was confiscated in Teush's apartment, the situation changed. It is one thing to hold at *Novy Mir* the manuscript of a novel already submitted by the author under contract; it is quite another matter officially to take into safekeeping the copy of a novel that has already been confiscated [by the KGB]. Solzhenitsyn did not give a damn for *Novy Mir;* consideration of Tvardovsky's position as the journal's editor simply did not enter into his calculations. An "underground" writer, as he himself attests, who had used such finesse in thinking up his secret hiding places, might well, it would seem, find his own place of safekeeping for his manuscript. To offer it to Tvardovsky in *those circumstances* was hardly an honorable thing to do; indeed, objectively speaking, there was more than a touch of the *agent provocateur* about it: If I'm caught and get into trouble, then let *Novy Mir* be caught as well—it will create an even bigger furor. And if you read this passage of *The Oak* very carefully, exactly what was the status of the manuscript that Solzhenitsyn was offering to Tvardovsky at that point? It was the second or third copy of the novel. One copy, as we now know reliably from the author (until then we only guessed it to be so) was hidden in the "underground"; another was already abroad. So that all the panic about the work being irrecoverably lost because of Tvardovsky's unwillingness to keep it in the editorial safe was unnecessary, and the comparison with Pushkin—who "wouldn't have refused"—is made purely for cheap effect and is actually based on falsehood. In other words, while I can fully understand Tvardovsky's attitude, I am wholly unable to comprehend the frenzied pique with which Solzhenitsyn accuses him of cowardice.

The second thing which makes Solzhenitsyn's picture of Tvardovsky unattractive is *vodka*. This being a delicate subject, I would much prefer not to write about it; but what is one to do when the topic has already been broached in *The Oak?* Solzhenitsyn sanctimoniously reproaches Tvardovsky for his predilection for vodka; like some lip-smacking Peeping Tom, he notes down Tvardovsky's drunken raving in Ryazan', whither he had himself invited him—"and that in the house of a writer who did not drink!" (p. 76). I find it painful and unpleasant to read these pages of the book.

The most obvious consideration simply does not enter his head: with Tvardovsky only four years dead, is it decent, while his wife and daughter are alive, to drag this unfortunate personal weakness into the open for the amusement of the reading public? In the last century this was called "personality," for which the culprit was excluded from the society of decent people; but the nineteenth century does not impress our genius—he has even taken Leo Tolstoy to task. Therefore I shall be rude too: supposing someone, in the role of virtuous moralist, were to start discussing the ins and outs of the personal life of "the calf" himself and to expose what is known about him from hearsay? Or started collecting the stories of his meanness and ingratitude from people who have helped him or are close to his family? "That's a very ungentlemanly way to behave," Tvardovsky, the peasant's son, used to say on such occasions.

Since, however, Solzhenitsyn has already stooped to this form of "ungentlemanly behavior," I should add a word or two on the subject. Yes, from time to time Tvardovsky did drink a great deal; he indulged in excruciating drinking bouts, and it must be admitted that adverse political circumstances were strongly conducive to this. With its excessive sensitivity, his poet's soul craved some form of defense against intolerable pressures. It is said that he became a really hard drinker during the war because he could not bear what he had to see—death, fire, his birthplace in Smolensk province reduced to ashes. And he drank equally hard during difficult times at *Novy Mir* when he sought and could not find a solution or protection both for himself and the journal. Solzhenitsyn is right when he says that vodka for him was a kind of escape. But he is wrong, insultingly wrong, when he depicts Tvardovsky in such a fashion as to make the reader doubt his moral health or the integrity of his personality.

I saw Tvardovsky at many different moments of his life; I myself downed more than one glass in his company, and I can say with absolute conviction that the amazing thing about him was that vodka did not destroy his moral self. Even when profoundly drunk he never confused his moral judgments, never said a word to hurt any person with whom he felt a sincere affinity, and he never expressed enthusiasm for anything that he would not praise when sober.

I remember another major poet, a contemporary of Tvardovsky's who suffered from the same problem; when *he* drank, it was impossible to talk to him or to sit at the same table. An evil demon awoke within him: he became peevish and intolerant, his talk was inane and filthy, he took pleasure in offending both friends and virtual strangers, and more often than not the affair would end in a drunken slanging-match. Nothing of that sort ever occurred with Alexander Tvardovsky.

Moreover, I was always surprised that even during his terrible drinking bouts his mind did not go to sleep and only got stuck in one groove more frequently than usual. He never descended to stupid, banal conversation, never took exaggerated offence over trivia in the way drunks do, and even in a haze of intoxication, when his tongue hardly obeyed him, he seemed to be thinking and talking about essential things which really mattered to him. To me this was one more proof of the integrity of his mind, the genuineness and sincerity of his emotions and desires.

In the drunken Tvardovsky as described in *The Oak*

I do not recognize the man who was close to me: somehow the picture is wrong. But Solzhenitsyn exaggerates and distorts this topic in a particular way which was not, of course, inspired by personal antipathy to Tvardovsky: he wants to show ". . . how unsteady, and how helplessly limp at times were the hands that managed *Novy Mir* . . ." (p. 78). He is thus echoing the usual slander put about by Tvardovsky's "official" detractors—that the journal was being run by an alcoholic, that his weaknesses were being exploited, and so on.

Solzhenitsyn's third accusation against Tvardovsky is even more obviously aimed not only at him personally but at the whole atmosphere in the offices of the journal—this is his accusation that there was a "cult" of the editor-in-chief, that he was excessively haughty, distant, and undemocratic. The author does not balk at such "artistic details" as the fact that Tvardovsky was nervous about crossing the street (implying that he was unused to going anywhere on foot!) or that he had difficulty in squeezing into [Solzhenitsyn's] old Moskvich (because ". . . in his position he was unused to riding in anything humbler than a Volga" [p. 73]—comments Solzhenitsyn). How utterly ridiculous! Tvardovsky really was nervous about crossing the street; he would grip his companion by the sleeve and was startled by any approaching car, but this was simply because throughout his life he never really got used to urban living: there was always a timid streak of the country dweller in him, which made him confused by the traffic and noise of the big city. I might add that he was made equally nervous by large expanses of water; when he and I were at Karacharov on the Volga, he felt unsafe when we got into a boat, like a person who has grown up far from a river (in his native region of

Smolensk there are no big rivers). And Tvardovsky had difficulty in squeezing into a Moskvich for exactly the same reason that when he was in my home he always preferred to sit in a wide, old-fashioned armchair rather than a fragile-looking modern chair: his stoutness—the man was broad-shouldered, solid, powerfully-built. How on earth can anyone interpret this as snobbishness?

Apart, however, from making tediously persistent references to Tvardovsky always finding "a long black limousine at the door" (p. 125) (the editorial staff of *Novy Mir* was allotted one Volga from the *Izvestiya* carpool, in which Tvardovsky used to go home or out to his *dacha*, which could only be reached by car)—Solzhenitsyn makes another, and more serious, remark: ". . . the editorial board . . . conducted its internal affairs on the basis of a personality cult of its own. . . . Tvardovsky's vision and his sense of humor were impaired, or he would have noticed the lingering frosts and dispelled them" (pp. 36–37). The editors of *Novy Mir* had but one aim—"to please the chief editor . . ." (p. 36). Throughout the book there are remarks about how inaccessible Tvardovsky was—how difficult it was for junior staff members to enter his office, how much depended on his mood, his whims, and so on.

It is a pity that an artist with such powers of observation and psychological insight is, in this case, so incapable of understanding people and circumstances, so relentlessly partisan that he paints a picture which is not merely distorted but completely upside down.

Tvardovsky was not a man who opened himself to anybody he might happen to meet. It is true that on strangers and slight acquaintances he often made an impression of introspective reserve, even of a certain haughtiness. Much, too, depended on his mood. But in none of this was there any element of posing or insincerity. His mind was ceaselessly at work, and being an essentially shy and sensitive man, he was afraid of unwanted interference. He was instinctively on his guard against impertinence, against intrusive and overfamiliar behavior. Yet, to anyone sharing his professional concerns—above all to anyone connected with *Novy Mir*—he was always open and accessible, even to people whom he did not particularly like, but who, in his view, were honestly doing their bit for the journal. When he was in his office, any colleague could go and see him at any time, and some of us abused this freedom. Moreover, *Novy Mir* was generally criticized for its free-and-easy ways and its organizational sloppiness. We had no regular editorial conferences, and when they did take place, as a rule no minutes were kept; in general the journal was run rather in the old Nekrasov fashion of the nineteenth century. The editor would arrive, fling down his battered yellow briefcase stuffed full of manuscripts and galley proofs—and immediately a gaggle of board members and editorial staff would gather around him. They would come with their questions, requests, and problems, and I know of no case when Tvardovsky refused to give anyone his attention, time to talk, and kindly advice. I have seen many editorial offices in my time, but such a lack of lordliness or office protocol, such unpretentious and natural egalitarianism I have never seen anywhere else.

But just as Solzhenitsyn applies makeup to the faces of people for his own aims—painting one person as an intriguer, another as a scoundrel, a third as a careerist—so too does he depict the atmosphere of the *Novy Mir* office in misleadingly somber colors. I need only recall Solzhenitsyn's remark that when one day he came to see Tvardovsky on business, all the staff members sitting in Tvardovsky's office immediately went out of the room, leaving them alone. Solzhenitsyn considered this to be "a mark of respect for rank" (p. 266), and nothing more than that. He did not see it as normal tactfulness toward a visiting author from out of town, one who was rarely seen at the journal, and who might have personal, confidential things to discuss with Tvardovsky (and I know that Solzhenitsyn always craved that confidentiality). Rather did he see it as "the basis of the personality cult" (p. 36), as "the logic of the officeholding hierarchy" (p. 97). It was from details such as this, alas, that Solzhenitsyn fashioned the whole of his depressing picture of the internal life of *Novy Mir*.

In his generally impressive description of Tvardovsky's leavetaking of *Novy Mir* of February 1970, when he went round to every room and said a few words of farewell to each member of the editorial staff, Solzhenitsyn stresses that until that moment Tvardovsky had never been on any of the floors except his own, ". . . he had never rallied at all . . . his staff around him earlier on" (p. 280). What an idiotic remark! We had all met together on a number of previous occasions around the table, whether it was covered with papers on a working day or decked for a party. Everyone who worked on *Novy Mir* in those days remembers the friendly warmth of those gatherings.

Solzhenitsyn alleges that the rank-and-file staff members who gathered in Tvardovsky's office after his departure exclaimed, as though overcome by emotion: "Let us forgive him his unjust persecution of us." What meaning, when applied to Tvardovsky, can this misquotation from Pushkin possibly have? Which employee over suffered from "persecution" by Tvardovsky? How could such a thought ever enter anyone's head? I have no idea; I am dumbfounded.

I do know, however, that in a certain sense a "cult of Tvardovsky," if you wish, did exist at *Novy Mir*—only not in the form perceived by Solzhenitsyn. Tvardovsky was immeasurably respected—both as a poet and as a man. The most varied collection of people worked for *Novy Mir*, but I cannot think of a single one who would have treated Tvardovsky without respect. The majority of them quite simply loved him, deeply and sincerely, trusted whatever he said and believed in his honesty. They respected in him his talent as an editor, his conscientious attitude to the job, and his scorn of empty formality.

For apart from everything else he was a *worker*. Who wrote the most precise, businesslike, and detailed replies to novice authors? Tvardovsky. Who made the best contributions—intellectually the most wide-ranging, the most demanding, the most precise in their literary perceptivity, the most brilliant in exposition—to our discussion of new manuscripts? Tvardovsky. Who was able bluntly and directly to tell an eminent writer, if he deserved it, that he had produced a failure? Tvardovsky. Who always found the warmest and most sincere words with which to congratulate a writer on a success? Tvardovsky. How could anyone fail to feel boundless respect for such qualities?

Solzhenitsyn gives us to understand that no one at *Novy Mir* dared to contradict Tvardovsky, with the possible exception of Dement'ev, who allegedly exerted an overwhelming influence over him. That also is untrue. People objected, argued and quarreled, and not once but many times. One who always expressed his opinion sharply and firmly—though never to the detriment of his personal friendship with Tvardovsky—was I. A. Sats. Zaks, Kondratovich, Gerasimov and others, each in accordance with his individual character, held views on specific matters of the journal's policy which did not correspond with the opinions of the editor-in-chief. About myself, Solzhenitsyn writes that he cannot remember a single occasion when I contradicted Tvardovsky in Solzhenitsyn's presence. That is understandable; in his *presence* I probably would not have argued with Tvardovsky. But to say "if I didn't see it, it didn't exist" is no way to interpret the real world.

It is with regret that I recall how many times Tvardovsky and I disagreed in our judgments on specific cases.* It even came to unpleasant, heated arguments. When roused, he would start shouting, and I used to walk out without a word. But the remarkable thing was that the next morning he would ring up as if nothing had happened; even if I had been in the wrong he was the first to ring, and would make a joke as a sign of reconciliation or would simply start talking business as if nothing had happened—and peace was instantly restored.

I have not yet mentioned Tvardovsky's own works—poetry and articles—which were offered to *Novy Mir*. He himself introduced an inflexible rule: in any discus-

---

* This occurred least of all with Solzhenitsyn's works. I had no reason to disagree with Tvardovsky when he praised *Ivan Denisovich,* "Matryona's House," or *The First Circle.* We also concurred in our criticism, chiefly on artistic grounds, of his play *Candle in the Wind,* on which Solzhenitsyn himself writes extremely vaguely. Solzhenitsyn gave Tvardovsky his poetry to read personally and, so to speak, "by the back door." Without benefit of a second opinion, Tvardovsky consigned it to the scrap-heap: "Don't even bother to read it," he told me (author's note).

sion of a work written by a member of the editorial staff, publication had to be unanimously approved by all the members of the editorial board. If there was only one contrary vote, then it would not be published—and he made no exception for himself. It needed only one doubtful or lukewarm opinion expressed by a board member for Tvardovsky to withdraw a poem. As for our arguments over his articles, there is evidence enough in the typescripts and proofs of his pieces on Bunin, Isakovsky, and others, where not a few of the remarks and corrections were my own.

That, briefly stated, was the true state of affairs with regard to the alleged "cult of Tvardovsky."

If while managing to say so much in *The Oak* that is unpleasant, false, and discreditable, Solzhenitsyn writes about Tvardovsky (according to some indulgent readers) with a certain sympathy, then his treatment of Tvardovsky's colleagues on the editorial board is ruthless. It is a gallery of monsters. Parasites, cowards, toadies and careerists "hanging on for dear life" to the arms of their editorial chairs.

This is how he writes about them:

A. I. Kondratovich—"a little fellow so mauled and terrorized by censors that his ears seemed permanently pricked up and his nose permanently atwitch for the scent of danger" (p. 20).

E. N. Gerasimov—"The complacent Gerasimov, a voluminous prose writer himself . . ." (p. 20).

B. G. Zaks—"asked only one thing of literature—that it not interfere with the comforts of his declining years: his sunny Octobers in Koktebel and his enjoyment of the best Moscow concerts in winter . . . indifferent as to the quality of any issue of the journal" (p. 20).

I. A. Sats—"his drinking companion, the bleary I. A. Sats" (p. 22).

A. G. Dement'ev—"a dependable ideological hoop . . . a dependable ideological lid" "a wild boar, inflamed with rage . . ." (pp. 28, 38).

To read these comments is like hearing the voice of Sobakevich.* Naturally these are all very different men with their own weaknesses and shortcomings, but in these malicious caricatures I do not recognize a single one of them.

"The complacent Gerasimov, a voluminous prose writer." Can this be Gerasimov—that unpretentious man, in his crumpled cap and grubby overcoat, permanently tousled and untidy, who only began to have his stories published when he was 60 years old?

"Indifferent as to the quality of any issue of the journal"—is this the Zaks who was boundlessly devoted to Tvardovsky and to *Novy Mir,* an indispensible expert on magazine publishing?

"Terrorized by censors"—this is said of Kondratovich, who for years obstinately and skilfully steered volume after volume of *Novy Mir* through censorship, each time honorably sustaining a battle with the censor of many hours' duration.

How can the brilliantly educated, witty yet extremely modest Sats—once the literary secretary of Lunacharsky, close friend of Andrei Platonov and Georg Lukács—be labeled "bleary"?

In his book Solzhenitsyn spared me to a certain ex-

---

* A figure in Gogol's novel *Dead Souls,* Sobakevich is a surly landowner characterized by his invariably coarse, foul-mouthed and uncharitable comments about all his neighbours and acquaintances. As a form of grotesque emphasis on the beastliness of his character, Gogol gives him a surname derived from the Russian word for "dog" *(sobaka)* (editor's note).

tent, in that he did not merely apply to me some dismissive catch phrase. He even did me the honor of analyzing my views, character, and "evolution" in a special "study" which, for obvious reasons, I will not discuss. But the spirit of all his remarks about the present writer is still that of Sobakevich's notorious remark: "They say that the public prosecutor is the only decent man in this town, and even he, if the truth were known, is a swine."

In other words, all the members of the editorial board, with the exception of Tvardovsky, are shown as largely devoid of "the insight, taste, or energy required to make serious literary judgments"; all were merely concerned "to pull and not to push," and represented nothing more than ". . . wooden dolls who were on the board for camouflage . . ." (p. 56).

How quickly Alexander Isayevich has forgotten some of our discussions of his work in which, among other matters, we discussed some of the literary shortcomings of this talented author. I remember how we reproached him with the improbability of a particular twist in the plot of his story "An Incident on Krechetovka Station," where his hero (an actor) did not know—in 1942—that Tsaritsyn had long since been renamed Stalingrad and thus aroused ultimately fatal suspicion of him in the mind of the young lieutenant. Everybody thought that this motivation was much too far-fetched. Many of us, too, objected to the way Avieta in *Cancer Ward* is drawn as a cheap caricature. We made many more "serious literary judgments," including some about his verbal experiments which were often remarkable but now and again were glaringly unsuccessful: new words full of vitality alongside artificial, stillborn ones. I remember that after one argument I gave him a copy of Preobrazhensky's

Etymological Dictionary, which no author should be ashamed of consulting to check on a risky word formation. There is much else to recall from our literary discussions, but the author of *The Oak* does not care to remember any of it, and suggests that Tvardovsky was surrounded by a gang of hair-splitting Jesuits and nonentities playing at backstairs politics.

There is therefore no need for surprise at his conclusion that for the creation of a journal such as *Novy Mir* it is not the editorial board that is responsible but ". . . the constant inrush of manuscripts from freedom-loving authors . . . ," manuscripts which, ". . . however many . . . were thrown out, however savagely they were mutilated . . ." (pp. 56–57)—something apparently the editors of *Novy Mir* did with particular relish—still contained much good material. One thing only is not clear: why has the "constant inrush of manuscripts" not produced the same effect in *Oktyabr'* or *Moskva?* Or does our author think that the editorial board, as he has described it, was unable, had it wished, to curb Tvardovsky's "liberal tendencies"?

There was actually a precedent for this in 1954, when during Tvardovsky's first editorship of the journal (1950–4) he had been forced to resign, while the editorial board, after "admitting its mistakes" and subjecting the editor-in-chief to criticism from several of the board members, continued working quite happily with the new editor.

The truth of the matter is that from 1958 Tvardovsky took particular care to choose his own editorial board. No one forced him to take these men, on whom Solzhenitsyn now comments with such scorn. Tvardovsky invited to the journal those people whose literary taste he trusted, whose political and moral convictions were close to his own. A majority of the editorial board members had been his friends and colleagues for many years, while men such as I. A. Sats or A. G. Dement'ev one may quite simply call his closest friends.

On the subject of Tvardovsky's friends, Solzhenitsyn denies him even this attribute, declaring that ". . . Tvardovsky had few, hardly any friends" (p. 22) that he ". . . was incapable of close association with his peers" (p. 57). This should read: he did not make friends with Solzhenitsyn, therefore he was incapable of having friends. It is absurd to have to explain and prove one's point in a matter like this, so I shall not go into any details of his friendship with Marshak, with Kazakevich, with Sokolov-Mikitov, with Isakovsky. . . . I shall just say this: if that marvelous comradeship which arose among us at *Novy Mir* in the circle of those who were close to Tvardovsky cannot be called friendship—then what does that word mean in any human tongue?

Why is it, I should like to know, that Solzhenitsyn depicts the life of the journal with such distortion and bias, with some sort of inner irritation and *Schadenfreude*? Why, in his description of Tvardovsky as editor, can I only rarely, in a few episodes, recognize the living Tvardovsky, and why do his portraits of people well known to me, Tvardovsky's close collaborators, look like malicious caricatures?

One reason is obvious: Solzhenitsyn did not know Tvardovsky well and he failed to understand him. During his visits to *Novy Mir,* when he was perpetually in a hurry, entirely self-absorbed, his observation of

what was going on in the editorial offices can only
have been superficial; and when he came to write
about it, with the uncharitable eye of a journalist looking for juicy copy, he seized only on its external features, misunderstanding a great deal of what he saw
and making a lot of judgments based on faulty guess-
work. In his book there are plenty of clues to his incomprehension of people and circumstances, even of
our conversations, which he registered when listening
with only half an ear and then recorded in the wrong
sense.

Here is a tiny example. Solzhenitsyn describes the
occasion when he and I drove out to Tvardovsky's
dacha. Tvardovsky was in a bad state, in the midst of
one of his drinking-bouts, and as he met us in the door-
way he turned to me with the strange words: "You see,
friend Mack, to what I have come" (p. 192). In the
context of Solzhenitsyn's recollections this phrase
sounds like a piece of weird, drunken gibberish, and it
is not surprising that after the word Mack Solzhenitsyn
originally put a baffled question mark. What indeed
can have induced Tvardovsky to call me that? On first
reading this passage, I too was nonplussed. What was
this hieroglyph? Then suddenly I understood. Solzhenitsyn goes on correctly to describe how I reacted to
Tvardovsky's words by putting my arm gently around
his shoulder. The point is that the author of *The Oak,*
as in several other instances, heard a sound and hastily
noted it in his memory or on paper and gave it an *interpretation* without understanding the real meaning.

Tvardovsky had a habit of using countless slang expressions, jokes, and funny quotations, which everyone
in our circle instantly understood from a single sylla-
ble, without the need to complete the whole saying. He

used, for instance, to greet a visitor to his office with
arms spread out in welcome and the words:

My house is getting full
Of crowds and crowds of people
Now tell me, if you will—
What news have you of *freedom?*

Or in reply to insistent questioning which he wanted
to avoid:

Let us guess, let us see,
What will Nicodemus say. . . .

"And Nicodemus says nothing," he would sometimes
add slyly.

So it was on this occasion that instead of a greeting
he paraphrased the words of Austrian general Mack
from Tolstoy's *War and Peace;* Mack was the unfortunate man who lost a battle and had to report to head-
quarters with his confession: "You see before you the
unfortunate Mack." With touching humor Tvardovsky liked to apply these words to himself in some of the
less happy moments of his life—to console himself and
others with a joke.

When reading *The Oak* I realized to my amazement
that Solzhenitsyn completely failed to understand
Tvardovsky's habitual, lively sense of humor, and
never caught the overtones of what he was saying. At
the same time, he took even a mildly ironic remark
with clumsy, flat-footed literalism. A good example is
his story of Solzhenitsyn's beard, to which he returns
several times with a sort of touchy irritation. I well remember the good-natured laughter in the editorial
offices which greeted this new adornment of Solzhenitsyn's features, and Tvardovsky inquired jokingly

whether this was meant as a disguise to elude the authorities and defect to America. It now transpires that Alexander Isayevich took this harmless joke with painful seriousness, as an expression of genuine concern that he really might escape—hidden behind his beard!

I recall meeting Tvardovsky on his return from Italy, where he had been with Surkov. On the return journey Surkov had stopped off somewhere en route, in Kiev if I remember rightly. "Where's Surkov?" I asked, not seeing him at the airport. "He chose freedom," said Tvardovsky with comic seriousness, and we split our sides over this joke, imagining Surkov asking for political asylum.*

Clearly, Solzhenitsyn is not very receptive to humor. This is one reason for his frequent misapprehension, resulting in a biased interpretation of many of Tvardovsky's remarks that he records in *The Oak.* "And what would have become of me without the Revolution?" (p. 31).—is made to sound like tasteless self-advertisement; "Emancipate me from Marxism-Leninism . . ." (p. 256)—like a piteous appeal; "I was away for two weeks on the banks of the Seine" (p. 127)—like hypocritical self-satisfaction. All three remarks were said with quite a different intonation (I can hear it now), and it seems quite pointless to misrepresent Tvardovsky as being stupider and shallower than he was even at his worst moments.

* The anecdote refers to a book by Viktor Kravchenko (d. 1966). Of Ukrainian origin, Kravchenko was an official of the Soviet Purchasing Commission in Washington, D.C., who sought political asylum in the USA in April 1944. His book *I Chose Freedom* (New York, 1946) became a best seller and its title came to typify the motivation of Soviet citizens defecting to the West—hence Tvardovsky's ironic joke about Surkov, a careerist literary bureaucrat, who is well known as a staunch Soviet loyalist.

In general, where Solzhenitsyn introduces remarks in direct speech, especially by people who are now dead, one is advised to treat them with caution. In one place, for instance, he cites the late Efim Dorosh, who is alleged to have made a mildly rude comment about me. I find it difficult to believe that he said it; it is too far from the truth and too much out of keeping with the relations that then existed between the extremely tactful Dorosh and myself. Solzhenitsyn, however, seems generally rather receptive to gossip, nasty rumors, and backbiting. He readily accepts them as the truth and strengthens them with the authority of the independent memoirist.

At this point I cannot avoid mentioning one individual among the *Novy Mir* staff about whom Solzhenitsyn has nothing but good to say. I refer to one of the editors in the prose department, Anna Samoilovna Berzer. Solzhenitsyn trusts her. We frequently find our memoirist quoting her as his source: "Knowing the ways of *Novy Mir* as she did, Anna Samoilovna reasoned . . ." (p. 19), and so on.

It is obvious from the book that Anna Berzer greatly exaggerated her own role when she gave Solzhenitsyn a retrospective account of the publication of *One Day in the Life of Ivan Denisovich,* and he believed her, believed in her boundless loyalty to him. She managed to convince the author that had it not been for her subtle feminine scheming "The editor's three guardian angels—Dementyev, Zaks and Kondratovich—would have gobbled up my Ivan Denisovich alive" (p. 21). After Berzer had read *Ivan Denisovich* when it was doing the rounds of the office in the routine "circulation file" and had been "amazed" by it, she took it upon herself "to manoeuvre it past the members of the editorial board," since she had no doubt that ". . . any member of the editorial board . . . would block the manuscript, sit on it, swallow it—anything to keep it out of Tvardovsky's hands" (p. 19). To her belongs the credit, in Solzhenitsyn's words, ". . . of landing it in Tvardovsky's hands first of all" (p. 19).

I do not want to deny the service performed by Berzer in spotting Solzhenitsyn's story and in making the initial appraisal of it, particularly since the author himself lays such stress on it. But anybody who was familiar with the workings of the *Novy Mir* editorial offices will confirm just how laughably distorted is the picture given here (as Solzhenitsyn himself confirms, from a story told to him later by Berzer herself).

Whatever consideration of editorial caution may have motivated Kondratovich, Zaks, and Dement'ev, they would never have concealed from the editor-in-chief a powerful and really interesting manuscript, even if it had no chance of ever being published. I, at any rate, can recall no such episode having taken place. Tvardovsky demanded unconditionally that he be shown any remarkable material in the "circulation file," and he would never have tolerated it if he ever found out that someone was "filtering out" a manuscript of this kind for political reasons. He read countless manuscripts which had no hope of publication, purely out of his insatiable personal interest in works by unknown writers of talent or commitment. And it is obvious to me that Zaks, Dement'ev and Kondratovich, *even if they did not recommend a manuscript for publication,* would never have consciously concealed it from the editor-in-chief but would have undoubtedly reported on it and given it to him to read.

Perhaps, though, they would have remained blind to the literary virtues of the piece? I doubt it. I often had differences of opinion on various editorial matters with Dement'ev and Zaks, but I would never deny that they both possessed a true flair for literary quality.

As for Berzer, it is true, as Solzhenitsyn remarks, that while Tvardovsky was prepared to acknowledge her editorial skills, he was not very fond of her, and—it now transpires—with good reason. Her ambitions were huge, her pretensions great—far greater than the modest scope of her actual job in the editorial offices. She never had to make responsible decisions, never had to fight for *Novy Mir*'s position against "higher authority" and the censorship, and therefore, perhaps, she saw the members of the editorial board around Tvardovsky as the chief enemies of "progress." As is now evident from *The Oak*, she felt no compunction at playing a double game; wishing to curry favor with authors at the expense of the editorial board, she fostered their apprehensions, created mistrust, spread rumors, and thus further complicated the position of Tvardovsky and of the journal.

Thus when Solzhenitsyn writes that during a long period in which he did not come to the editorial offices ". . . it was only from Berzer's accounts that I got to know what was happening at *Novy Mir*" (p. 34), it is obvious how biased and unreliable was the source of his information. Even so, what is important is not the information itself. The principal factor is the angle, the viewpoint, the position from which that raw material is cooked up and presented—and here, of course, the responsibility for giving it this or that interpretation belongs entirely to the author, especially since we have a right to expect a genuinely profound and independent understanding of people and ideas from someone gifted with an artist's insight.

As I write all this, I am thinking about Solzhenitsyn;
I recall him as I knew him in the 1960s and I wonder:
surely we cannot have failed quite so badly to understand him? Was he faultlessly playing out a role of his
own and fooling us? Or is he now dissembling and was
he, at the earlier stage, a rather different person?

I remember him as a modest Ryazan' schoolteacher
in a plain Russian shirt with rolled-up sleeves and
open collar; I remember his energetic efficiency, his
firm handshake, the unexpectedly cheerful, open smile
that would light up his otherwise rather glum features.
He seemed to be untouched by the seduction of sud-
den world wide fame that burst upon him: he was firm
in his convictions, but tolerant and patient, straightforward, cordial in his relations with slight acquaintances . . . and does he now expect me to agree that
all that was a pose, a mask, playacting?

Yes, toward the end of the 1960s he did begin to
change somewhat. He acquired a more dignified bearing, and a tone of peremptory self-assurance crept into
his voice with increasing frequency. The miserly attitude toward time, which even previously had been one
of his ingrained characteristics—always on the move,
always in a hurry, always glancing at his watch—grew
into a fussy preoccupation with haste, which expressed
itself in a lack of attention to whoever happened to be
talking to him. At the time, one overlooked these
trifles. Now, with hindsight, I see in them more clearly
the logic of changes that were taking place within Solzhenitsyn himself.

Solzhenitsyn seems to think that in the seamless, all-
of-a-piece figure which he has created of himself there
should be no place for change, for evolution. He entered into literature, it would seem, ready-made, and,
at least since the day when he crossed the threshold of

Novy Mir, he has not changed but has merely been putting his own secret plan into operation. That is not true. He has changed, and his plan has changed too. Even after reading his autobiographical "legend," I at any rate am left with the definite impression that in 1962–4 he was not simply utilizing circumstances for his own ends but was sincerely trying to "grow into" Soviet literature and public life, and that, despite his highly critical stance, he at least did not reject various forms of contact with it. Although unwillingly, he did make compromises in order to be published: he wanted to please (and did please) the country's top leadership; he attended receptions given by the Central Committee's Secretary for Ideology, and was prepared to accept a Lenin Prize as a deserved reward. . . . From one slip of the pen in *The Oak* we learn that in 1963 the author, on returning to Ryazan' from one of Khrushchev's meetings with writers and artists, gave a report on his impressions of the event to a gathering of writers and other prominent local figures. The presiding body on this occasion included the Ryazan' "secretary for ideology," who later faced Solzhenitsyn at the meeting which expelled him from the Union of Soviet Writers (pp 260–262). In other words, there was a time when he too behaved—for better or worse—in the same way that the majority of Soviet writers behave.

Nowadays, he either remains silent on many of the items in this set of facts or presents them in a different light. But I sometimes think that if the leadership had adopted a more sensible attitude to him, if they had not prevented him from getting the Lenin Prize in 1964, if they had allowed *Cancer Ward* and *The First Circle* to be printed in the Soviet Union—we should today see Solzhenitsyn as a very different person. One must give him his due. For a long time he showed a certain flexibility and tolerance in his dealings with the Union of Writers, he did not reject the possibility of reasonable compromises, and it is not his fault that the authorities failed to meet him halfway. A writer is an extremely private, egocentric sort of creature, and this was not understood by those people whose job it is to be aware of it. They rejected him and made him their bitterest enemy. I remember Tvardovsky giving a similar explanation of what happened with Solzhenitsyn: "They harassed him and harassed him to the point where he wouldn't take it any longer and slipped away from their grasp."

Of course Solzhenitsyn, with his insatiable pride, would never agree with that interpretation. He thinks that he was always the same as he is today, and that his whole subsequent career was already lying mapped out, as it were, on a scroll of paper in his pocket; his autobiography is supposed to illustrate this. The book about the calf took a long time to compose; it was written at various times, was completed abroad, and it bears the traces of hasty work—there are corrections, patching, and erasures which were obviously made with hindsight and were necessary in order to make the whole thing hang together. Like the stories of other people in his book, Solzhenitsyn's own story has been doctored in order to bring it into line with his final conception.

I have had a fairly long and close acquaintance with the writing fraternity and in part belong to it myself. Therefore I can confirm that with few exceptions all authors, especially those who have inhaled the fumes of fame, are ambitious and as eager for praise as children; they cannot bear the slightest criticism, are vulnerable, biased, and egocentric. Solzhenitsyn, however, is not just a writer; he is a great writer, endowed with colossal talent, with shattering energy and will power, which have themselves become part and parcel of that talent and have enabled him to survive and establish himself amid extremely unfavorable circumstances.

Equally great—bordering on ridiculous folly or raving arrogance—is his sensitivity to both abuse and praise, his consciousness of himself as the center of the universe. "His poor old skull couldn't stand the strain," was Tvardovsky's comment on the effect of fame on Solzhenitsyn.

In *The Oak and the Calf* he has made the fatal step from the sublime to the ridiculous. It is painful to say so, but its author is even ridiculous when he observes with satisfaction that "God had spared me creative crises, fits of despair and impotence" (p. 7); also when he says that for many years "I was not mistaken about a single person or a single event" (whereas his entire book is a catalogue of misjudgments and disappointments over people), and when in refusing any gratitude to Tvardovsky for the publication of *Ivan Denisovich*, he announces that "Troy after all, does not owe its existence to Schliemann . . ." (p. 51).

"Troy does not owe its existence to Schliemann"— what an aphorism! Our Troy does not suffer from an excess of modesty, either; but keeping to the terms of this picturesque analogy, I feel I must defend not only Tvardovsky but Schliemann as well. Were it not for that German genius, Troy would have long remained unrevealed to our age, perhaps might have never been discovered at all, just as dozens of other forgotten centers of civilization slumber beneath the earth and the waters to this day. As for the fate of Solzhenitsyn, I fear that [without Tvardovsky] he simply might not have existed at all as a writer. He could, of course, have consoled himself with the thought that "those whom I reached by some invisible flow would accept me." He would have been left with the hope of that "invisible flow" and nothing more. And if by happy chance his secret writings did survive for future generations, they would probably have been of interest—as he himself put it—only to some "gravediggers" from the journal *Moskva* in the twenty-first century.

"Manuscripts do not burn." But the trouble is that by the twenty-first century *Ivan Denisovich* and Solzhenitsyn's novels would be of little more than academic, historical interest. Art is long-lived, but nonetheless in literature it is an advantage when the "discovery" of a writer takes place at a timely moment, when a book forms part of the living organism of society. So it is perverse of our Troy to be angry with his Schliemann and to reproach him with not having shown sufficient haste in excavating him from the tumuli of obscurity.

Nowadays, after a lengthy period in which the attention of Europe and America has been fixed upon him, after his tours as a celebrity and his speeches at formal banquets in his honor, the Nobel laureate's self-image has somewhat changed. Now that he is floating free, as it were, in boundless outer space, he is anxious to forget that his first boost of orbital speed was given to him by Tvardovsky's journal. Yet without *Novy Mir*, either he would never have overcome the drag of terrestrial gravity or he would have been burned to a cinder in the denser layers of the atmosphere. His self-intoxication leads him to imagine that his progress—both yesterday and today—is the spontaneous movement of his genius, a flight path determined in advance by Providence.

The fact is that Providence and Solzhenitsyn are on

the most intimate and confidential of terms. Since the early 1950s he has come to believe in miracles and in a divinely ordained aim for his life. Even when adapting *Ivan Denisovich* for publication, he was doing it on inspiration from above: "I had never known what prompted me to 'lighten' *Shch-854,* or what purpose it could serve . . ." (p. 16), and Tvardovsky the unbeliever never guessed that he was the blind instrument of Providence when he decided to publish the story. Later, too, Solzhenitsyn found that "Something has always set me on the true path" (p. 111) in all his actions, and he discovered a secret meaning in his life—a discovery which "dumbfounded" him.

When one is so aware of one's mystic predestination and has such a messianic sense of divine Providence at work within oneself, life is never dull: henceforth any whim, any off-the-cuff political comment, any prompting of self-will, can be regarded as the mysterious voice of heaven and one can always justify oneself. A convenient and very modern psychological device! It does not even involve the attempt, as was the case with A. S. Khomyakov, to make the distinction between "Divine will" and "Divine acquiescence." Henceforth, we are supposed to be aware that everything which Solzhenitsyn writes or does has the sanction of heaven and his judgment is infallible.

Unfortunately, Solzhenitsyn's God bears too little resemblance to the Christian God, with his commandments to practice lovingkindness and self-denial. Solzhenitsyn's God is rather more like that Supreme Being, who is worshipped in the abstract, and whose authority is acknowledged by Dostoyevsky's Grand Inquisitor in the attainment of his worldly aims. At the same time, in addition to the notion of divine authority, Solzhenitsyn employs two more of the Grand

Inquisitor's concepts: *miracle* and *mystery*. By "miracle" is meant the divinely preordained aim of Solzhenitsyn's life, which he is busy acting out, while "mystery" is the guiding principle of his personal behavior.

"I can recall nothing in my own activities over the years of which I would ever have spoken in advance except in strict confidence," writes the author of *The Oak*. "Whatever effect they had was the result of secrecy and suddenness" (p. 374). What is remarkable about Solzhenitsyn is that he not only keeps things secret from his enemies but, as far as possible, from his friends, allies, and those who share his views.

It does not seem to matter that the promptings of intuition are not always correct. When Solzhenitsyn got angry with *Novy Mir* for failing to publish him over a long period, he concealed from Tvardovsky that he was making secret overtures to the journals *Ogonyok* and *Moskva*. After trotting back and forth between the offices of Alexeyev and Sofronov [the editors of *Ogonyok* and *Moskva* respectively], he returned empty-handed to the "dull-witted tutelage" of *Novy Mir*. Unable to forgive his humiliation, he abused *Novy Mir* again for good measure, complaining that he had been kept too long in "*Novy Mir*'s fetters," and that if he had gone to Sofronov first, it might have been more successful. Solzhenitsyn describes all this with calm self-confidence, without a flicker of embarrassment on his face; shame is something that only other people feel.

"They cannot hear their own words," as Akhmatova used to say in such cases.

I must add, however, that our author most certainly *sees* himself, or rather he ceaselessly admires himself in his self-created literary mirror: "I felt myself, saw myself, making history" (p. 145), he remarks unblushingly. This perception is spelled out in the details of his self-portrait. Here is our hero entering Tvardovsky's office: "I entered the room looking cheerful and pleased with life, and was met by a subdued and dubious Tvardovsky" (p. 152); and this is how he makes his appearance at the Secretariat of the Writer's Union: ". . . with an inscrutable face, in the voice of one intoning truths for the ears of history, I hurled at them my first statement . . ." (p. 182). Who else has ever written about himself like that in his literary memoirs?

Solzhenitsyn has no doubt that in his dealings with *Novy Mir*—as in everything else—*he was always right,* and that is the greatest weakness for a thinker wishing to demonstrate his strength. What is more, if anything in the past does not fit in with his present-day perceptions, then he erases that past event from his memory and from his writings. He must be somewhat embarrassed by the avowals that are scattered throughout his letters written in past years to Tvardovsky and the editorial board. "Personally I have never known anything but kindness from *Novy Mir*," he wrote to me, for instance, in 1970. Were it possible, he would doubtless rewrite those lines, just as in Orwell's grim utopia old newspapers are retrospectively reprinted in order to bring them into line with the changing political imperatives of the present day.

As he observed Solzhenitsyn's "dodges," which became more and more noticeable as time went by, Tvardovsky said with his wry grin: "Why does A. S. always have to be so devious? Why all this conspiratorial secrecy? Why am I not allowed to know his address? Suppose I want to send him a telegram. . . . He's a rum bird, and no mistake; Marshak has nothing on him!" (Samuil Marshak, the poet and translator, was notorious for his obstinacy and prima donna-ish whims.)

Solzhenitsyn carefully concealed from Tvardovsky and the rest of us the existence of his little house in the country near Kaluga. "I kept my hideout at Rozhdestvo a secret, especially from *Novy Mir*" (p. 204), he now admits. However, even Homer nods, as the proverb has it. He thought his hideaway was a secret until one afternoon Victor Louis* descended on him, brandishing a camera; it transpired that the whereabouts of his residence, so carefully concealed from us, had for long been known to all the sparrows that chirrup in the lime-trees outside the Lubyanka.

Despite the numerous misunderstandings resulting from this secretiveness, Tvardovsky was far from suspecting all the permutations of the double game which Solzhenitsyn was playing with us. I generally defended Solzhenitsyn in front of Tvardovsky, whenever a quarrel threatened to break out, while to Solzhenitsyn I tried in amicable fashion to explain Tvardovsky's position and to arouse his sympathy for Tvardovsky. It always seemed to me that a public break between the two would be a great misfortune for literature, and by reasoning with each of them separately I did what I could to keep tempers cool.

But if we had known then what Solzhenitsyn was later to say in his book! It appears that he realized—not at once, but still in time—that in his dealings with *Novy Mir* he had to adopt ". . . the defensive cunning

---

* Vitaly Levin, alias Victor Louis, a Soviet journalist with close links to the KGB; implicated in, among other shady affairs, the transmission abroad of the manuscript of Solzhenitsyn's *Cancer Ward*, an action which prevented its publication by *Novy Mir*. Victor Louis is the Moscow correspondent for a group of British newspapers (editor's note).

necessary in all dealings with authority" (p. 67). During the very first discussions of *Ivan Denisovich* he sat there looking reserved and ". . . so nearly grim" [because] "I had chosen to play this part" (p. 24).

All right, that was understandable; he didn't know the *Novy Mir* staff very well, so he indulged in a bit of playacting. But when without a trace of an ulterior motive, in all frankness and genuine enthusiasm, we asked him what else he had written and whether we might publish it, he dissembled, prevaricated unnecessarily, concocted artificial and misleading replies as though he were facing a police interrogator. He deliberately tried to impress us with his poverty—a teacher's salary of 60 roubles a month. He now admits in his book that he did not want to draw more than a half-time salary because he was living well enough on his wife's much higher earnings. And how depressing it is to read that even a photograph, taken in the autumn of 1962 and used for the cover of the serial publication of his novel, bore the marks of his calculated playacting: ". . . all that mattered to me was my expression—one of exhaustion and deep sorrow—and this we managed to convey" (p. 48).

He dissembled, as he now admits in *The Oak*, even in his letters to Tvardovsky. He wrote him a letter, for example, that he "pretended was written from the forest of Ryazan' " and addressed Tvardovsky as the first person to have read his novel. "Like hell he was the first person to read it!" Solzhenitsyn then adds by way of comment. "I continue to follow the activities and the policy of your magazine with complete approval," he goes on in the same letter. "This, of course, was stretching it a bit" (p. 151), he now hastens to correct himself.

As late as 1969, when *Novy Mir* was in deep trouble,

Solzhenitsyn said to Tvardovsky: "If for the good of the journal you have to disown me, then do so. The journal is more important." I remember the look of round-eyed perplexity on Tvardovsky's face when he repeated this to me. Solzhenitsyn had left him nonplussed rather than delighted. To suggest that we should disown him, disown *Ivan Denisovich*—did he realize what he was saying? We were of different mettle. Besides, even then Solzhenitsyn was pretending and playing games: if he could say something like that, it meant that he could equally well say something quite different. He gives himself away in another sentence, after describing a heart-to-heart talk with Tvardovsky in the editorial offices about the fate of *Novy Mir* (1969): "I said goodbye. We had talked like bosom friends—and all the time I had had a knife in my boot. I could not possibly have shown it to him; it would have ruined everything" (p. 268).* And that was the way—"with a knife in his boot"—that the author of *Ivan Denisovich* talked to his literary godfather, his mentor, and practically his only strong and loyal defender in the writers' world. For years he lied, dissembled, and prevaricated to the people who trusted him, played a false double role without apparent reason or necessity; he was, I suppose, lying "for the good of the cause." And is that what he means when he now calls upon us "not to live by the lie? †

* Solzhenitsyn's remark about a "knife" refers to his *Open Letter to the Secretariat of the Union of Writers* of 12 November 1969, in which he protested vigorously against his expulsion from the Union (editor's note).

† "For the Good of the Cause" is the title of one of Solzhenitsyn's stories published in *Novy Mir* in 1963. "Not to live by the lie" is the title of a polemical article in which Solzhenitsyn exhorts his fellow countrymen to abandon their tacit or active acquiescence in the falsities, hypocrisy, and deceit on which the social and political structure of the Soviet regime are based (editor's note).

The Solzhenitsyn of today dictates laws to mankind, calmly announces to the American people his approval (or disapproval) of their politicians, and explains to them what their interests are in various corners of the world. When making his pronouncements in the West, he generally does not speak for himself but in the name of the Russian people, or the suffering intelligentsia, or the fighters for freedom—in the old Soviet manner of only speaking "in the name of" or "on behalf of." Nowadays, however, I would not risk saying, because I simply do not know, when he is genuinely telling the truth according to his convictions and when he is playacting, consciously striving for effect, or simply being hypocritical.

In one of Chekhov's stories, the merchant Tsybukin put a number of counterfeit coins into a chest full of gold; the false pieces looked so much like real money that it was impossible to distinguish the gold coin from the fakes. After that, his worst nightmare was that now he would think all the gold coins in the chest were false. This is the effect of *The Oak and the Calf.*

Before finishing with this subject, let me give just one more picturesque psychological detail. Solzhenitsyn complains that in the last year or two of [Tvardovsky's editorship of] *Novy Mir* I was of little help to him, on such occasions as when he asked me to arrange for him a meeting with Tvardovsky or to fix up something else that he needed. ". . . Lakshin, with his discreetly limited aims, must think my influence on Tvardovsky ruinous. Ever since *Ivan Denisovich* I had been used to thinking of Lakshin as my natural ally. But this had long ceased to be so" (p. 242).

What a fascinating thing human psychology is! He conceals his intentions from me and does not trust me, yet he gets angry because I refuse simply to act as his blind tool. I am supposed to persuade Tvardovsky to meet him, but as to what the meeting is about—mind your own business. It is not surprising that this exploitative attitude was hardly calculated to arouse a surge of enthusiasm in me at our last meetings. Tvardovsky was direct, sincere, and comprehensible in his feelings and actions, and by contrast Solzhenitsyn's dodges and twists looked peculiarly out of place. For a long time in my heart of hearts I discounted the nagging feelings of distaste which Solzhenitsyn's behavior evoked in me, and I tried to explain away his tactlessness as the foibles of genius, eccentricities whose meaning I preferred not to examine too closely in order not to be disillusioned.

I see now that Solzhenitsyn's attitude toward other people as mere means to gaining his ends—in other words, the very opposite of what Kant declared to be the only indubitable criterion of morality—has become second nature to him. He only believes and trusts those who follow him unquestioningly. The truth has been revealed to him; he is leading us toward the light and no one is supposed to ask questions—we must *believe* in him. If Solzhenitsyn summons us to humility and repentance, then naturally everyone must repent except him; his vocation is to absolve us from our sins. Solzhenitsyn does not recognize equality in matters spiritual.

That is why, I think, with all his tremendous gifts of artistic insight, he is doomed to be perpetually disappointed in other people, to live in a world of illusions and phantoms and to be hopelessly prone to error in his judgment of broader political perspectives, because his criteria derive only from himself and his immediate circumstances.

When *Novy Mir* was publishing him (or was able to

publish him), *Novy Mir* came first for Solzhenitsyn; later, when he launched his writings into the stream of *samizdat*, then nothing was more important than *samizdat;* now *samizdat,* too, has little significance compared with foreign publication. And if Solzhenitsyn were to land on the moon tomorrow he would regard setting up a lunar printing press as the most important task in the universe.

I pause, and I wonder: perhaps all this is unimportant, insignificant or forgiveable when compared with that vast and terrible truth which Solzhenitsyn has uttered in his best works? Are we here faced with the age-old dilemma of how to reconcile the small lie with the great truth, greatness of spirit with ingratitude, "genius" with "villainy"?

Is the answer to the riddle perhaps to be found in the psychology of the prison-camp inmate? "[My skills] are those of *katorga* and the camps . . ." (p. 272), writes Solzhenitsyn. These skills, as his book makes clear, are as follows: if you sense danger, anticipate the blow and strike first; pity no one; tell lies with ease and wriggle out of trouble; throw up a smoke screen to escape an awkward situation (he recalls the proverb: "He who fights and runs away lives to fight another day"); finally, adopt the habit of always believing the worst of others.

Solzhenitsyn's behavior is not the behavior of a calf, but of a prison-camp wolf, and one must give him his due: his character and his acquired habits undoubtedly helped him to survive in camp and, once at liberty, to fight his particular battle. The only trouble is that the means are not compatible with the end. Or are we once again doomed to affirm the truth by means of a lie, to instill good by force and to inspire belief in the power of honesty while rejoicing in the skillful use of deception?

Solzhenitsyn is inclined to regard prisoners as a special tribe, posessing their own psychology, morals, and language. My respect for these people, for their misfortune and their tragic fate, is boundless. Suffice it to discover that a person went through the horrors of Stalin's prison camps, that he served out his term of eight, ten, or fifteen years (or, like Dmitry Vitkovsky, half his life)* for those of us of another generation who escaped that fate to pull ourselves together and treat that person with the special degree of sympathy and respectful admiration due to someone who endured such suffering. Among my acquaintances, close friends, and correspondents, are many remarkable men who did their stint in Magadan, Kolyma, or Ekibastuz. I have seen them just after their release from prison camp, and I have seen them at later stages; they have all absorbed the experience of the camps in different ways, and they have returned to "real life" without the slightest trace of prison camp cruelty or arrogant scorn for those who were "outside." So the tribe of former prisoners is not, to say the very least, uniform in character.

Indeed, are all the members of that tribe alike even in prison? Solzhenitsyn himself, in his description of camp life in *Ivan Denisovich* (I mentioned this very

* Dmitry Petrovich Vitkovsky (d. 1970). An engineer by profession, Vitkovsky was arrested on political grounds in 1926, in 1931, and again in 1937, spending a total of over 30 years in various prison camps. Released under Khrushchev's amnesty, Vitkovsky wrote his memoirs, entitled *Half a Life*. Tvardovsky signed a contract with Vitkovsky to publish this book in *Novy Mir*, but was never able to do so. Extracts published in issue no. 1 of the journal *Dvadtsaty Vek (Twentieth Century)*, London, 1976; pp. 138–236.

point in an article I wrote in 1964) has shown to perfection that all the mechanisms of human relationships that functioned in "free" society were reproduced—albeit in ugly, distorted, horrible forms—
inside a prison camp. There, too, people behave in different ways—there are the noble and the servile, the
good and the evil; and there, too, in an environment
where the prisoners have all been, it would seem, reduced to a common level of degradation by their misfortune, there emerges a sort of hierarchy, with relationships of dominance and subservience, and a whole
gamut of small privileges. Indeed, it could not be otherwise; people took into the camps the habits with
which they had been imbued outside, and they
brought back their accumulated prison-camp experience when they returned to "freedom."

I say this because Solzhenitsyn himself, it seems,
does not realize quite how much of his prison-camp
education, of which he is so proud, is the purely *Stalinist* element of the camp ethos that permeated the in-
mates: indifference to means, the psychology of the
preventive strike, cruelty, and lying. Having been
rightly schooled in hatred of Stalinism, without realizing it Solzhenitsyn also imbibed the poisons of Stalinism; is that not surely the reason why his book contains so much intolerance, malice, deviousness, and
ingratitude? Objectively speaking, of course, this crip-
pling of the moral character of a man of great talent is
one more item to be counted against the Stalin era.
But in the end we are judged by our actions, and the
paradox is that the author who addresses us with his
passionate appeal for us to pursue truth, humanity,
and goodness scorns to observe these commandments
in his own dealings.

While loudly condemning all forms of violence, in

particular revolutionary violence, Solzhenitsyn does not seem to notice that he himself is fostering the idea of a war to the death, ridiculously aping his antagonists even in their predilection for military phraseology. We know how much writers of the Kochetov school * love the roll of drums, and we know how fond they are, even in time of peace, of peppering their books with militaristic jargon for home consumption. More than once *Novy Mir* had occasion to ridicule this habit in its reviews. It was therefore all the more distressing to discover the same stylistic device being used in *The Oak*, the same method of whipping up passions through the militarization of the vocabulary of social and literary discourse: ". . . I gave them a hundred-and-forty-four-gun salvo . . ." ". . . the field of Borodino . . ." "The battlefield is in their hands!" and so forth (pp. 182, 183, 184)—one feels embarrassed for Solzhenitsyn that he should describe his encounters with the Union of Writers in these terms. Amid the fumes of powder smoke and the roar of toy cannon, one's confidence in the narrator is eroded and melts away.

One can understand an author being especially proud of *Gulag*—not as a book, but as an accusation and a weapon. It is undeniable that despite all the illusions of its author, this literary investigation will have a long life. It is a bill of indictment, a speech for the prosecution containing countless passages of invaluable testimony, and a passion for revealing the

* Vsevolod Kochetov (1912–76) was editor-in-chief of the journal *Oktyabr' (October)* from 1961 until his death. His novels, stories, and articles invariably gave enthusiastic, even exaggerated support to the ideology and policies of the Soviet Communist Party (editor's note).

suppressed truth—together with much exaggeration bred of hatred. Until history finds more objective chroniclers and pronounces its own judgment on the past, Solzhenitsyn's biased judgment will stand—both as a memorial to those who perished and a denunciation of the Stalin régime.

But I fail to understand why, without waiting to hear what others may have to say about it, he has to describe his own work in these terms: "of lethal power," "a crushing blow," "a book like the stroke of a scythe." And still more absurdly: ". . . the blood must have turned to ice in their veins: such a publication might [?] be fatal to their system" (p. 360); ". . . I had been thundering against them for seven years now" (p. 398).

It is no exaggeration to say that from 1966 to 1974 the author won his battle with his persecutors and beat the propaganda machine; as a result, he has been somewhat intoxicated by his victory. Yet it also seems that this victory was won at the cost of considerable losses. To write about oneself as Solzhenitsyn writes in *The Oak* can only be done if the writer holds a certain view of himself: as if, in fact, he were standing at the hub of the universe and dictating its laws. Nothing exists for itself, but only in relation to him; all benefaction is bestowed by him and his curse alone is enough to reduce everything to dust and ashes.

But the aim, the aim! What is the aim, the end to which all these questionable means are directed? Perhaps the end justifies everything, redeems all means; perhaps our complaints are no more than futile, petty grumbles, pinpricks at a genius who has been bold enough to look ahead into our future?

Ah, if only that were so!

Solzhenitsyn presents himself in *The Oak* as a man with a clear program. He has always, on every occasion since the end of the 1950s, known what he wanted and has devoted everything to one cause, one aim. What is it? His personal aim—the publication of his "underground" works—he has fully revealed and brilliantly achieved, although even here he retrospectively ascribes to himself rather too much foresight. It appears that mentally he had already even awarded himself the Nobel Prize, of whose existence he first learned in the prison-camp; at that very moment, apparently, he decided: ". . . this was just what I needed to make my great breakthrough when the time came" (p. 290).

Apart, however, from a personal aim—praiseworthy though it undoubtedly is—a man who plunges headfirst into a political struggle must have a more general aim, one which concerns the present and future welfare of his people, his country. And here—despite apparent clarity—total vagueness reigns. What does he want for Russia, what does he expect from her? I don't know; I cannot make it out. Judging by his idyllic conception of our prerevolutionary past, he seems to think that Russia's only future is . . . her past. One has but to read his "Letter to the Soviet Leaders" to find that he has no objections to a strong and rigidly centralized government, while even autocracy and great-power manners have a certain attraction for him. If the Soviet leaders would only listen to Solzhenitsyn's good advice and abandon their pernicious ideology, all would be well. If in addition they would revert to a national, established Orthodox Church, then . . . from the fog of verbiage there now clearly emerges the triad proposed by Count S. S. Uvarov: "Orthodoxy,

Autocracy (now replaced by strong Soviet state power) and the National Principle." *

Dissatisfaction with the present draws Solzhenitsyn back to the past, making him idealize the old Russia; but whether he likes it or not, that Russia has long since passed away. People live differently, think and feel differently, pray to other gods (or do not pray at all), and no amount of nostalgic looking back at 1913 is going to make them change their way of life.

What does he expect of the future? What can he offer? Fierce genius of negation, he has no clear idea of what to propose, no positive conception of what his fellow Russians should hope for. That is why he is so easily seduced by spur-of-the-moment political expedients, random recipes for salvation, such as the proposal to accelerate the opening-up of the northeast—(by whom? By a new injection of convict labour? Who will go there of his own free will?)—or by our leaders voluntarily surrendering their ideology to the Chinese.

This typically amateurish, fragmented, improvised political thinking is yet another consequence of a do-it-yourself education. Never having been able to make a systematic study of philosophy, history, or sociology, Solzhenitsyn is convinced that on the strength of his admittedly exceptional abilities he can simply leap over all difficulties in any branch of knowledge at one bound. Hence his susceptibility to being dazzled by what are, for him, blinding flashes of revelation. He has never, it seems, made a thorough reading of Her-

* Count Uvarov (1786-1855) was appointed Minister of Education by Nicholas I in 1833, after submitting a report on Russian universities, in which he enunciated the 'three principles' that should bind the Russian people into a loyal unity with tsarist autocracy (editor's note).

zen or Chernyshevsky,* and his references to them
sound distinctly schoolboyish, imprecise, and undi-
gested. As for Tolstoy and Dostoyevsky, he obviously
read them a long time ago and without close attention.
Otherwise it is hard to see why he has suddenly seized
upon Vekhi † as though it were a new gospel, seeing in
this book (brilliant in its way but profoundly retro-
grade, woven out of the efforts of several philosophers
of very unequal worth to rethink their ideas) the very
last word in irrefutable truth.

There were, of course, a number of points on which
Novy Mir saw eye to eye with Solzhenitsyn. We too dis-
liked the Soviet brand of centralized, bureaucratic socialism; we defended humane justice against dry dogmatism; we were appalled by the horrors of the Stalinist prison camps and protested, whenever we could,
against the many subtle forms of social and political
hypocrisy practiced in the USSR. But we believed in
socialism as a noble ideal of justice, we believed in a
socialism that was human through and through and
not just with a human face. We regarded the democratic rights of the individual as incontestable. We
sought support for our feelings and convictions among
the people, and while abhorring the cheap, phony pathos that so often mars the use of that expression, we
always cherished the awareness of a common cause

* Alexander Herzen (1812–70), the theorist of Russian non-
Marxist agrarian socialism, or Populism; a gifted and influential
writer on revolutionary politics. Nikolai Chernyshevsky (1828-89),
a radical thinker and publicist whose writings on society exerted a
strong influence on the political thought of Lenin (editor's note).
† *Vekhi (Landmarks)* was a collection of articles published in Moscow in 1909. Its contributors, themselves mostly ex-Marxists, attacked the socialist and materialist beliefs held by a large proportion of the Russian *intelligentsia* and called for the adoption of an
essentially religious approach to social and political thought
(editor's note).

with working people. This was simply second nature to Tvardovsky.

It is undeniable, of course, that any great idea can be distorted in its historical application, sometimes to the point where it becomes unrecognizable. Is this the fault of man's "original sin," of his genetic immaturity as a species, of a lack of receptivity in his moral consciousness to new forms of life, or is it due to the rotten, polluted soil of antecedent social influences and traditions? Whatever the cause may be, any step toward a humane improvement of the social structure is made only, it seems, with extreme difficulty, and it is fraught with backsliding, disappointments, and potential catastrophe.

Solzhenitsyn would like to remake the world, to re-create it to his own design. For him, socialism has failed to pass its test. As a principle, an idea, he is inclined to reject it root and branch and to replace it with . . . what? There's the rub.

May it not be, in fact, that all the woes and failures of our country have arisen precisely because we have interpreted socialism in an archaic, monarchical fashion in accordance with just those ancient Russian traditions that are so dear to Solzhenitsyn? After all, even though the idea of socialism, which came to us from the developed West, was buttressed by the instinctive habits of our peasant commune, it nevertheless fell on a soil that was so arid, so weighed down with centuries-old traditions of slavery, so poisoned by the age-long rule of the St. Petersburg bureaucracy that the very idea itself. . . . But that is altogether another question. "Pitfalls abound for us if we're to take that way," as Count A. K. Tolstoy once said, rhyming it with the next line: 'Far better to keep silent and not to say our say." * What is important to stress is that *Novy Mir* fostered in its readers the ability to think, to perceive the reality of their situation and to strive for better things. The journal cultivated a sense of continuity with the traditions of democracy and culture—a mainly educational task, but one which for our country is both important and broad in scope.

For the author of *The Oak* none of this exists. He wants to speed up time; he cannot wait, he nags at those who have not yet seen the light, he hurls accusations of cowardice and pettiness at everyone who is not totally on his side or who does not rage blindly at whatever displeases him. Therefore if *Novy Mir,* in his view, had any justifiable aim at all, it was simply to support him, Solzhenitsyn. There was a time—and not so long ago—when he talked seriously about "moral socialism" (in *Cancer Ward*). Now he rejects this; those were merely the words spoken by one of his characters. For Solzhenitsyn personally, socialism is now a swear word. That being so, and since he can offer no positive alternative to socialism, the only thing he can do is to keep expanding the scope of his destructive criticism by arraigning history, like the dealer in a card game who is perpetually raising the stakes. Yesterday, everything was the fault of Stalin; today Lenin is the culprit; tomorrow it will be the whole of nineteenth-century Russian society and its thoroughly atheistic literature, and the Decembrists, and Herzen; and then before we know where we are it will be the *philosophes* of the French Enlightenment who are to blame, and then Descartes, and then Aristotle, and then God

* Quotation from a long satirical poem entitled *History of the Russian State from Gostomysl to Timashyov* (1833) by Count Alexei Konstantinovich Tolstoy (1817–75), poet and playwright; cousin of the novelist Leo Tolstoy (editor's note).

knows who else among those who have ever tried to inspire respect for thought. Why bother to make any distinctions? They're all tarred with the same brush. Thought itself is the evil; the sole good is faith.

If only there were someone who could help us to believe in Solzhenitsyn's God! In all frankness, I simply cannot sense anything really resembling God in Solzhenitsyn's system of belief. I cannot detect any sincerity in his faith, just as I find it hard to believe in Solzhenitsyn as a politician and a thinker, even though he has already acquired all the attributes of a familiar type of politician—with his insatiable urge to anathematize, to reject, and to demand of his supporters nothing less than an oath of total loyalty. I doubt whether Truth will be vouchsafed to us through him and I don't want to be in his paradise; I fear I would find myself in an ideally organized prison camp. I don't believe in his Christianity, because no one with such a misanthropic bent and such self-worship can possible be a Christian. And I am fed up with his hatred and rejection of everything in present-day Russia.

But surely, I hear people object, hatred has its attractions. True. Sermons on virtue soon grow tedious. Uttered by some boring, discredited public figure, the debased coin of speeches about Truth, Goodness, and Justice rings hollow and insultingly trite, especially when in fact everything is in disarray and confusion. And then the genius of evil appears and speaks out in the admirable, appealing guise of noncomformity: his destructive words of truth have an unexpected charm and are avidly imbibed. Time is needed for people to become sated with his speeches, for the green mold of banality to start to show through and for his hearers to regain the firmness of their original belief in good. It is these unpredictable, spontaneous swings of opinion

among the educated public, from one pole of attraction to another, that go to make up the repetitive history of political belief and disenchantment.

Unfortunately, if one leaves out of account the enormously attractive power of his destructive arguments,
all Solzhenitsyn's positive ideas are fragmentary, random, un-thought-out and thrown off on the spur of the
moment, carelessly and irresponsibly worded. Making
the most of the uncertain, flickering limelight of popularity, he talks and talks and talks, with growing malice toward his own country and the people who remain
there without him. Roosevelt's mistake, we are told,
was to grant diplomatic recognition to the Soviet
Union. . . . Another mistake was to support the
USSR in the war against Hitler . . . And now—there
should be no trade, no sale of grain, no détente, if necessary at the risk of war. . . . He thinks he is fighting
against "the régime," against "ideology." But is he
not, in fact, fighting against the millions of people who
inhabit his own country? *Pereat mundus et fiat justitia!*
Everything must be reduced to ashes if it does not con-
form to Solzhenitsyn's views, his ideas, and his
criticism—and no one, nothing is to be spared. Let
there be no bread, let there be hunger and war; but let
there be no mercy for "ideology." In the Soviet Union
it is probably only the most dogmatic, hard-line *ap-
paratchiks* who exhibit such blind attachment to their
ideas and who push them, like Solzhenitsyn, to their
most extreme and inhuman conclusions. (Is this not
somewhat reminiscent of the case of another Nobel
laureate, Jean-Paul Sartre, doggedly marching on in
his blue Mao tunic when the world had long since
learned to ignore what he was saying?)

Solzhenitsyn ascribes all the ills of Soviet society to

ideology, without realizing that today—as at all times—ideology is to a great extent a derivative of real human life—which ought to interest us, at the very least, as much as ideology itself. Here, by the way, I am making use of what is undoubtedly a Marxist concept, and Solzhenitsyn fears Marxism like the devil, seeing its pernicious traces in every evil or even every stupid act. This is not the place to discuss the actual significance of Marxism for human history, beneficial or destructive. I shall only remark that what currently passes for ideology in the USSR today contains so much that is hollow and purely ornamental, lifeless detritus that only rustles like last year's unswept leaves, that it is doubtful whether "Soviet ideology" any longer has much in common with Marxism. But that is by the way.

In his most recent articles Solzhenitsyn has been heaping abuse on our intelligentsia (calling it "an educated rabble"), in which he points out a good many of its real shortcomings. He also refers without any great sympathy to "the people," whom he tends to see as an amorphous mob. But the root of all evil, or so he thinks, is still "ideology," which has turned everyone's brains askew. His fears are misplaced. What he calls ideology is, in fact, more often than not mere phraseology, a sort of vacuum which is filled as the need arises. With us, Marx and Lenin have long been among the most unread of authors. There is no sign that the "leadership" has ever read Marx at all (in general, they prefer reading typewritten reports and "extracts" summarized for internal Kremlin circulation). Marx and Lenin are even less popular among large sections of the intelligentsia. For a long time now Soviet life has followed its own particular line of development and keeps going, for better or worse, by inertia, only now and again seeking an appropriate [Marxist-Leninist] quotation to suit some occasion.

It is a pity that Solzhenitsyn's extremist temperament seeks out the wrong fulcrum at which to apply its force, and that he himself falls so easily into dogmatism and intolerance. True, he has shown us an example of his readiness for self-immolation that is worthy of Avvakum.* He tells us in *The Oak* that in order to ensure the publication of *Gulag,* he came to the ". . . superhuman decision . . ." that, if necessary, he would sacrifice his own children (p. 360). Dostoyevsky would have shuddered to hear that. What is this? Is it the highest form of self-abnegation? Or is it, perhaps, the ultimate in callousness?

Having turned moralist and politician, Solzhenitsyn at once loses sight of ordinary people with their everyday interests, their weaknesses and their strengths. It is, of course, true that people ("the population," as [the Stalinist bureaucrat] Rusanov calls them in *Cancer Ward*) are very imperfect and are inclined to make compromises because they yearn for a quiet life. Anyone is liable to be plunged into the deepest pessimism if he expects ordinary people, after hearing a few words of high-minded preaching, at once to start acting reasonably and virtuously—and then he finds that they do not. Instead, to keep one's equilibrium one must know and believe that in ordinary people—sinful,

* Avvakum (1620 [?]–1682) was an archpriest of the Orthodox Church who refused to accept the ecclesiastical reforms of the Patriarch Nikon, and became the spiritual leader of the schismatic sect known as the Old Believers. For this, he was imprisoned underground for fifteen years and, on still refusing to recant, was executed by being burnt alive. His *Life of the Archpriest Avvakum* (1672–5) is the first autobiography in Russian literature (editor's note).

inconsistent, clumsy, naive and experienced, untouched or scarred by life—there is a great deal that is good, despite their day-to-day conformism, their opportunism, and their failings. This is the optimistic view. Otherwise, the preacher has no recourse but to nurse his angry disappointment with the frail humans who perpetually fail the tests this stern moralist has set for them.

To act fairly is always, in the final analysis, to achieve a synthesis between the interests of others—the social principle—and one's personal interests. Even in his social behavior, however, Solzhenitsyn is highly personal. And so, to return to the depiction of Tvardovsky and *Novy Mir* in *The Oak,* it is apparent that Solzhenitsyn at first regarded the editors of that journal as his potential enemies, who had to be twisted around his finger in order that *Ivan Denisovich* might be published. Later, when Tvardovsky published this work and *Novy Mir* started to defend Solzhenitsyn against the stupid attacks on him, he began to think that perhaps we did share his views, only that out of cowardice or cunning we would not admit to it: "Ever since *Ivan Denisovich* I had been used to thinking of Lakshin as my natural ally . . ." (p. 242). Then, when we could no longer publish him, disillusion overcame him again—("But this had long since ceased to be so.")—and he started talking about my "limited aims," hinting at their selfish and personal nature. As I have already mentioned, he treated Tvardovsky's other coeditors without a trace of indulgence.

He was unable to imagine that people with socialist and democratic convictions could be genuinely interested in such fearless criticism [of the system] and show such concern for literary talent. As far as Solzhenitsyn was concerned, there was only one alternative to his genius—official intolerance and a hypocritical, lying press.

There was, therefore, a fundamental division between us, and it is not surprising that he failed to understand or acknowledge the main principles of our cause.

It is painful for those who admire and respect Solzhenitsyn's talent to see what has become of him. But it is worst of all for Solzhenitsyn himself.

Has he not exploded the edifice of untruth? Yes, he has. But he has become an infernal machine, convinced of its divine mission, which has started to blow up everything around it. I fear that he will also blow himself up—indeed, is already doing so.

I am not sure how right William Blake was when he wrote:

A truth that's told with bad intent
Beats all the lies you can invent.

There are cases when the truth can only be spoken in anger. But how are we to understand the phenomenon of Solzhenitsyn? We read his short stories and novels, and we are thrilled by them: what a knowledge of the human heart, what omniscience, what a dispensation of the artist's higher justice! . . . But in that case, why does he display such meanness in *The Oak*? Whence this spite and ingratitude? And where is the dividing line between the divine discontent of genius and the autocratic whims of an evil man?

With all my heart I wish him a recovery of his moral good health and a new impulse to his art, but to judge by his most recent pronouncements the prognosis is unfavorable, as the doctors say. He has done an immeasurable amount for all of us and for Russian literature—for which unending homage to him. Yet the evil demon of destruction, the prison-camp virus, has gone on the rampage within him and is threatening him, for all his worldwide fame, with a future of terrible, wolfish isolation and loneliness. "You want freedom for yourself alone," Tvardovsky once said to him with bitter humor, quoting the words of Pushkin's gypsy.*

It has pleased fate to teach us all two lessons through the example of Solzhenitsyn: first—the lesson of the unprecedented courage which has enabled Solzhenitsyn to overcome all obstacles and to win his battle; second—the lesson of the sterility of his passionate hatred and arrogance.

There is only one explanation: Solzhenitsyn is the offspring of our terrible century, the prodigy who has absorbed all its inspiration and its degradation, its suffering and its burdens. As well as the best and loftiest of human qualities, his psychology also bears the stamp of the concentration camp, of war, of totalitarianism and the atomic bomb—the chief features of this age.

In *The Oak,* Solzhenitsyn cites his own letter to Tvardovsky, in which he says: ". . . [as a writer] I belong to the Russian convict world no less . . . than I do to Russian literature" (p. 272). The observation is true, not only in a good sense but also in a sense that can only inspire regret. Is it conceivable that a writer of the

---

* A quotation from lines spoken by an old gypsy in Pushkin's poem *The Gypsies* (1824). Aleko, a Russian fleeing from justice, joins a gypsy troupe and is accepted as one of them by the peaceful gypsies; unable, however, to adapt to the easygoing gypsy code of live and let live, he kills his rival in love. For this he is bitterly reproached by the old gypsy and is banished from the troupe (editor's note).

Russian nineteenth-century tradition could show such relentless egocentricity, such coldness toward others, such messianic fervor, such blind inability to perceive the legitimacy of any interests that happen to conflict with his own, such remorseless bellicosity?

Of course, both Dostoyevsky and Tolstoy (and we are justified in measuring Solzhenitsyn with the same yardstick as these two) were also egocentric, but they at least wrestled as best they could with their selfish natures by constantly examining their own behavior and reproaching themselves for their own shortcomings. Hundreds of pages of Tolstoy's diary are devoted to scourging his human weaknesses, as he tried to correct himself by a constant application of his theory of self-perfection. Solzhenitsyn has switched off this kind of compensating mechanism: he regards his own egocentricity as legitimate, and sees himself, like the engineer Kirillov in *The Possessed,* as a man-God. Pity, compassion, justice, empathy, nobility of soul, gratitude—the further he goes, the less he feels any need for these qualities.

The unprejudiced reader will no doubt be amazed by an episode described in *The Oak* and which occurred during the last, most difficult months of Tvardovsky's editorship of *Novy Mir.* Solzhenitsyn received a telephone call to say that ". . . Tvardovsky was in a terrible state! He was asking for me! He was prepared to wait all day!" Solzhenitsyn reflected and decided: "I wasn't a first-aid team." (p. 272). And refused to go. How, after that, can he talk about good, comradely relations"? How can he preach Christianity?

It is true that among Russian nineteenth-century writers there were several men of genius who espoused some disastrously wrong-headed theories and pursued ideas that led them into many a blind alley. Even Tolstoy and Dostoyevsky were often bad prophets whose sermons grew more and more narrow-minded and uncompromising as their fame increased. Dostoyevsky insulted the Jews, grossly flattered Pobedonostsev* and mourned the loss of the Dardanelles. Tolstoy rewrote the gospels in his own manner and insisted that everyone should practice sexual abstinence within marriage. No one, needless to say, obeyed them; no one, apart from a handful of blind adherents, followed them. Yet none of this prevented mankind at large from regarding them as mentors—but in a different, broader, more elevated sense, in keeping with the fundamental ideas which they expressed through their literary works. From the giants of Russian culture Solzhenitsyn has inherited not only a proneness to cherish vexing and ridiculous illusions, but also their schoolmastery tone of voice. "To hell with the philosophy of the great men of this world!" Chekhov once exclaimed, referring to Tolstoy: "All great sages are as despotic as generals, and they're as rude and tactless as generals, too, because they are so certain of their impunity." What is somewhat worse, however, is that Solzhenitsyn is now starting to break with certain fundamental moral traditions which underlay the literature of the past. His spleen, his intolerance, and his vanity have reached such proportions that they are blinding him. If there is one tradition that he echoes in his recent autobio-

---

* Konstantin Pobedonostsev (1827–1907) was the teacher and later the adviser of Czar Alexander III. As Procurator of the Holy Synod from 1880 until his death, he used his influence to promote the most reactionary forms of absolutism and blocked all attempts at reform. Under the tutelage of Pobedonostsev, Alexander III's reign was politically repressive and marred by a series of pogroms against the Jews (editor's note).

graphical writing, it is perhaps the tradition of Vasily Rozanov, with his cult of hatred, his indiscriminate contempt, his morbid self-love and his cold scorn for people and morality.* The difference between them is that Rozanov did it first and with more originality: while there was something repellent in his alternation between acting the *enfant terrible* and indulging in grotesque self-adulation, he was never so pompous or so ridiculous as Solzhenitsyn and he did at least redeem himself by his genuine, if pathological, sincerity.

In the light of the foregoing, it becomes easier to understand the extraordinary episode in which Solzhenitsyn—during the first few months after Tvardovsky's removal from *Novy Mir* and the enforced dissolution of his editorial board—actually offered his support to the journal under its new editor, V. A. Kosolapov. Solzhenitsyn let it be understood that if he could be published, he would as willingly be published by Kosolapov as he had been by Tvardovsky, and he encouraged other writers to take the same line.

In 1970 I was shattered by this apostasy. Now, having read *The Oak,* I am, if anything, more amazed at my own naïveté. For at the time when he was making verbal declarations of his loyalty to Tvardovsky, in his heart of hearts Solzhenitsyn had long since held a different view: ". . . the struggle between *Novy Mir* on the one hand and *Oktyabr'* and the whole "conservative wing" on the other reminds me of nothing so much as the surface tension between contending forces, together creating a film through which the livelier mole-

---

* V. V. Rozanov (1856–1919). An original if uneven writer, he propounded an eccentric and inconsistent "philosophy" based on the deification of sex as the prime motor of human conduct. Flouting all conventional religious, social, and political beliefs, whether of the left or the right, Rozanov enjoyed a considerable *succés de scandale* in his time but is now largely forgotten (editor's note).

cules down below cannot break out" (p. 121). (Phew! As I was copying out that quotation, I thought to myself: how badly that is written, how untypical of Solzhenitsyn's style; it reads as though he had suddenly lost his ear and his good taste.) Or, somewhat more picturesquely: if *Novy Mir* was a window, "It was . . . a warped window, crudely hacked in a rotten wall . . ." (p. 122). Forgetting that it was precisely through *Novy Mir* that he burst out from the depths of obscurity, our "lively molecule" has no compunction in comparing Tvardovsky as an editor with Safronov or Alexeyev; what is more, he plainly shows a preference for Safronov's entourage at *Ogonyok*—people like Kruzhnov or Ivanov—over Tvardovsky's closest colleagues at *Novy Mir*.

Why was Solzhenitsyn dissatisfied with *Novy Mir*? In order to please him, it seems that the journal should have published material that was "of the ultimate degree of audacity"; every issue, according to him, should have been put together ". . . without reference to the mood of the day among top people . . ." (p. 56). It is not for me to assess the degree of boldness and independence shown by *Novy Mir*; that is better done by others. Considering that *Novy Mir* was an organ of the Union of Writers, whose 150,000 copies per issue went out under the vigilant gaze of its readers from above and below, and that it was printed on the presses of *Izvestiya*, it would be absurd to contend that it was totally independent. The question is—given that dependence, did *Novy Mir* retain its dignity, its integrity of purpose, the quality of its contents, its honesty? I believe that with only minor exceptions, the journal faithfully lived up to Tvardovsky's criterion: "I don't think we shall be taken to task in the next world for not having done what we *couldn't* have done; but if we *could* have done something and didn't—for that we will be punished." Within the bounds of what was possible, *Novy Mir* did virtually everything that it could have done to sustain the confidence of its readers in literature and in its capacity for telling the truth. Of prose writers alone, the journal attracted, nurtured, and supported, apart from Solzhenitsyn, a whole generation who were the glory of our literature during the 1960s: Vasil' Bykov, Vasily Belov, Chingiz Aitmatov, Boris Mozhayev, Gavriil Troyepolsky, Vasily Shukshin, Vladimir Tendryakov, Yury Dombrovsky, Konstantin Vorobyov, Yury Trifonov, Sergei Zalygin, Georgii Vladimov, Vladimir Voinovich, Vitaly Syomin—the list is far from exhaustive.

The authority and popularity of *Novy Mir*, however, was not only founded on its publication of stories, novels, and poems of greater or less quality. The journal provided an intellectual and moral *level*, and in this respect it acted as a prop and support for its readers, as a certain sort of objective model or standard. The letters which came to the editorial office in huge quantities confirmed that for many people in the 1960s *Novy Mir* became a part of their personal existence: it inspired a faith in the indestructibility of the truth, it helped people to live, and it fortified a sense of human dignity in the consciousness of hundreds of thousands of our fellow citizens. The journal both reflected and formed public opinion. Its readership extended far beyond the circle of Moscow's intellectual élite or the impressionable young. *Novy Mir* was read in the corridors of power, in remote villages, and in the most distant provinces, and its readership spanned laborers on construction sites, librarians, village schoolteachers, agronomists, passionate lovers of truth and lonely seekers after faith. As they opened the pale blue cover of a new issue it was as if they were hearing a familiar voice, one which was listening to their thoughts, sharing their feelings, not lying to them, striving to reassure them and, without talking down to them, sharing new ideas and problems with them.

The mere existence of a *Soviet* journal of this unique kind was, if you like, a modest embryo of democratic socialism, which gave an impression, if not of the norm (we were always far short of that) then of a movement toward the norm. Under Tvardovsky's editorship, the bitterly criticized but unsinkable *Novy Mir* was for many people in our country the pledge that evolution toward a healthier society was possible—a society with a worthwhile literature and a high level of self-criticism, and one in which the voice of public opinion would not be gagged. Six years after its suppression, the lack of such a publication is painfully obvious, not only in literature but in the whole of Soviet life. Nothing has succeeded or replaced Tvardovsky's *Novy Mir.*

When Solzhenitsyn reproaches the journal with having been insufficiently bold, this reeks of extremist demagogy. It should not be necessary to recall that Tvardovsky had neither his own printing press, his own compositors, nor his own paper; that every sheet of page proof was scrutinized and stamped by the censor (in the later years, in fact, by a whole team of censors), who would pepper the copy with so many red pencil marks that it made one literally see red when reading it; that the printers automatically refused to typeset any page that was not stamped and counter-signed, and that no amount of "audacity" on the editor's part could have circumvented this rule; that the journal, whose issues often appeared a month or two late, would simply never have seen the light of day at all if, having overrun every possible deadline, having appealed to highly placed officials and having written angry protests at the censors' arbitrary behavior (how many of them Tvardovsky wrote!), the editors hadn't replaced the contentious matter with other material, often no less significant, thus wearing out the censor by sheer attrition. In short, if Solzhenitsyn had been the editor of *Novy Mir* for a month or two, with his ideas of audacity he would never have published a single issue of the journal, so that under his editorship there would simply have been no question of some unknown mathematics teacher from Ryazan' getting into print with a manuscript such as *Ivan Denisovich.*

Alas, *Novy Mir* was never able to publish many works that were accepted and announced as forthcoming, yet which never got beyond the galley proof stage: Alexander Bek's novel *The New Appointment,* Nikolai Voronov's story "The Wrecked Taxi," Azolsky's novel *Stepan Sergeyevich,* Konstantin Simonov's *War Diaries for 1941,* and Tvardovsky's own poem *By Right of Memory.* It is quite likely, by the way, that even if the journal had published everything that Solzhenitsyn wanted, its level of boldness still would not have satisfied him: for that, *Novy Mir* would have had to have concurred in all his political views and to have followed wherever he led—and both Tvardovsky and the rest of the editorial board were far from being always in agreement with Solzhenitsyn.

Then after setting such impossible standards for *Novy Mir*'s publication policy, after displaying such Robespierre-like maximalism, Solzhenitsyn suddenly exhibited an astonishing indifference to the official dispersal of the editorial board and Tvardovsky's enforced resignation. He made no public protest at the news; on the contrary: in conversation with other writers and in letters to me he attempted, with hindsight, to accuse the old editorial board of weakness and inconsistency. He actually considered that we had deserved our fate, and he proceeded effectively to offer his support to the journal under Kosolapov.

It does not need much imagination to realize what this meant to Tvardovsky at the time. Even though Solzhenitsyn was not acting wholly independently, having swallowed the self-justifying arguments of certain female members of the editorial staff who stayed on to work under the new editor, his position astonished Tvardovsky and the rest of us. How could he? To be accepted, to be published, to smile at us, thank us, assure us of his sincere sympathy—and then when the board was dismissed to stab us in the back. . . . For a long time we simply could not take it in.

Having mounted that horse, he had to gallop on. Next he peevishly scolded Tvardovsky for his hierarchical cast of mind, his undemocratic behavior. He who prides himself on never seeking advice from anyone before taking action upbraided Tvardovsky for not calling a meeting of the junior personnel of the journal and consulting them on what to do before his departure. With biting sarcasm (but completely without foundation) he ascribed to the dismissed editors of *Novy Mir* the authorship of certain anonymous panegyrics to Tvardovsky which made their appearance in *samizdat* on the day after the breakup of the board. And he even sneered at Tvardovsky's terrible disease, whose cause is tragic and only too clear, suggesting that it was a consequence of Tvardovsky's cowardice: "Cancer is the fate of all who give themselves up to moods of bilious, corrosive resentment and depression"

(p. 285). In other words, it was his own fault that he got cancer, because he gave in to his moods . . . moods brought on by Tvardovsky's years of daily wrestling with stupidity, moral thuggery, and calculated falsity, of insults borne with stoical fortitude and patience, of newspaper attacks and officially imposed delays and stoppages in the publication of his books. To all this was then added the treachery of people who were ostensibly the best friends of *Novy Mir* and of some who only yesterday had been his colleagues.

Tvardovsky was never joking when he used such words as honor, truth, and courage; when he paid for this with his death, it was not so that Solzhenitsyn could sneer at him about it beyond the grave.

It is clear to me that for Solzhenitsyn the death of Tvardovsky provided a means of making a public appearance and of showing off under the spotlight. Stricken by our loss, we all failed to realize this at the time. The only thing that struck us as odd was Solzhenitsyn's reply to Tvardovsky's younger daughter, who invited him to make his last farewell to her late father in the small mortuary at Kuntsevo, where only close friends were to assemble on the eve of the funeral and where there would be no pomp and no crowds. "No," replied Solzhenitsyn, "my whole day is already planned. I'll come to the lying-in-state at the Central House of Writers tomorrow, as I have already noted in my diary." And he arrived, having skillfully stage-managed his entrance and attracted a horde of photographers—insolent, sweating with zeal, behaving offensively by standing with their backs to the casket and firing off flashbulbs point-blank at Solzhenitsyn as he sat in the front row alongside the widow, hastily scribbling his impressions of the ceremony in a notebook and preparing to make his theatrical farewell gesture—with a kiss and the sign of the cross—to the man who could no longer answer back to him.

I know how painful many people will find it to part with their idol Solzhenitsyn. For a long time he was the embodiment of our courage, our conscience, our ability to face the past fearlessly. But what are we to do when that idol turns out to have feet of clay? We must learn to live without it.

I have kept silence for a long time. I have been silent when I should have spoken. To speak now—as I bid farewell to Solzhenitsyn—causes me much pain. Many writers and intellectuals still want to see Solzhenitsyn as a prophet of a new heaven and a new earth. Whatever he may have said, and whatever we may think of it, it was bold, daring, destructive, and it answered our unspoken need for someone to raise their voice on our behalf. He has avenged our humiliation, our silence, our acquiescence, our compromises with our own conscience. He spoke when we were dumb.

People in Russia are reading *The Oak* with trust and with passionate interest. Why? Because it is brilliantly written? No; not counting a few pages that are marked by Solzhenitsyn's sustained intensity, it is not up to this author's standard. Out of interest in writers' lives, in the literary world, in portraits of the famous people described in it? No; it is not that either, but something else.

The Soviet intelligentsia is going through a difficult time: we are now, it seems, immeasurably far away from those thrilling years of 1956 to 1961, when the Stalinist "cult of personality" was denounced, when there began the whole cleansing process implied by that vague phrase. Today, to the incessant drumming of routine official phraseology (which no longer even seriously tries to convince anybody but is inculcated by sheer repetition, like army drill), lassitude, apathy, and indifference have gripped a noticeable proportion of the intelligentsia. At times like this, marauders rifle the dead.

In the last years of his life, Tvardovsky recited some lines of verse to me, which I quote here from memory:

It is as though our time's grown hollow:
What filled it once has gone,
And even what we hoped would follow
Will never now be done.
The body lives today, tomorrow;
The soul from it is gone.

In the literary world people respected Tvardovsky and were even a little afraid of him, but it cannot be said that he was universally liked, and for this reason *The Oak and the Calf* turned out to be timely. The black seed fell on receptive soil. During his lifetime, Tvardovsky was a permanent reproach to the very many outwardly law-abiding but inwardly nonconformist people who might be called crypto-liberals. He had never been in a prison camp; on the contrary, he had been favored and accorded official honors. Yet in the years of his editorship he had changed to being more liberal than any of them, had sacrificed everything for *Novy Mir* and for the common cause, and had died morally undefeated. That is why, among the people who by one means or another will get hold of Solzhenitsyn's book, there will not only be those who will read it with disappointment and mistrust, but others who will seize on it eagerly and with burning interest. Solzhenitsyn's peevish spleen suits them: yet another "liberal" reputation has been destroyed. It is, after all, gratifying to be able to say to oneself: "No one can hold up *Novy Mir* as a shining example to me any longer; I wasn't the only one who was a coward and a weakling. Look at Tvardovsky—what price his courage and his independence now?"

Solzhenitsyn has played up to exactly this kind of thinking. He could not bear the thought that in the eyes of the world he would be ranked alongside another great reputation—that of Tvardovsky and his journal—and so he has hastened to denigrate it. This is an obvious example of a psychological condition which may perhaps be called the Hercules complex. It is essential for everyone to know that he conquered the Nemean lion and the Lernean hydra unaided. No one was at his side! He is beholden to no one! He alone fought the good fight and won! This display of naïve, ridiculous self-aggrandizement will doubtless be seen for what it is, even by the most credulous readers.

I get angry with Solzhenitsyn when he libels Tvardovsky or others who are close to me. But when he writes about himself, I pity him. I pity him for the loss of his sense of proportion, for his childish boasting, his absurd degree of blind self-assurance. Although there are plenty of things in his memoirs to make one smile, I shall restrain myself from holding him up to ridicule.

His name is linked with too much that is powerful and valuable in our literature and the history of our civic consciousness. His rash political judgments and his faulty predictions will all sink into oblivion; books like *The Oak* or his articles in *From under the Rubble*—"ad-hoc literature," to use Solzhenitsyn's own expression—will be forgotten. But his main works, the books written on his great theme—*Ivan Denisovich, The First Circle,*

Cancer Ward—will stand and will outlive us all. That is why I pity him, sincerely and with grief.

For an abandoned temple—is still a temple. . . .

I say once again and for the last time: the significance of this writer is immense, the destructive and cleansing power of his best books is immeasurable. Added to his literary talents he possesses monstrous energy, diabolical vanity, and an incredible capacity for work. He has banished from himself many truly Russian weaknesses—from vodka to simple human pity. In his personal and public life he is practically a superman, a genius born of the twentieth century who measures up to it in stature. Yet I believe that an artist is not a superman, not a man-God, but is simply and above all a man; and if he lacks the truly human qualities and attributes, this is bound to show through, and soonest of all in the naked prose of autobiography.

"Why do you regret the loss of Byron's diaries? To the devil with them!" wrote Pushkin to his friend Vyazemsky. "Thank God they are lost. He confessed his true self in his verse, involuntarily, carried away by the inspiration of poetry. In cold-blooded prose he would have lied and dissembled, either in trying to astound people by his sincerity or in trying to blacken his enemies."

I don't know how true they are of Byron, but I am inclined to apply these lines to Solzhenitsyn.

When life gets intolerable and I need to be reminded of a man truly sublime and generous of spirit, I always think of Tvardovsky. And I am convinced that the cause for which he gave his last years—*Novy Mir*—will always be held dear by men of good will.

One day, books will be written about it, books that are nothing like the distorted, self-serving memoirs contained in *The Oak and the Calf.* Then, rising above all the ephemeral rancor, the exaggerations, and the egotism, it will be made clear to the literate world how *Novy Mir* served a cause that was honest and universally important, and how truly great was the powerful, original, attractive character of its editor.

Moscow, 9–30 August 1975

Alexander Tvardovsky:
A Biographical Study

Mary Chaffin

When Alexander Trifonovich Tvardovsky was first named editor of the journal *Novy Mir* in February 1950, he was already acknowledged to be one of the most popular contemporary Soviet poets. His first great success had come in 1936 with the publication of *Strana Muravia (The Land of Muravia)*, an epic about an itinerant peasant slowly becoming reconciled to the reality of collectivization. Ten years later, the publication of *Vasily Tyorkin,* a product of his experiences during the war, was received with great public and critical enthusiasm. The next year *Dom u dorogi (The House by the Road)* earned him another Stalin Prize.

Tvardovsky's stature as a poet may come as a surprise to those in the West who have seen him as a political figure, as a champion of the "liberalizing," destalinizing impulse of the late 1950s and the 1960s. As a matter of fact, almost any of the labels commonly used to describe individuals within the Soviet system (Stalinist, liberal, hack, dissident, and so on) could be applied to Tvardovsky at some time during his career. For he was a person who combined a tremendous capacity for personal growth and an ability to reconsider long-held opinions with a loyalty to and identification with the forces and circumstances that shaped his early years. Born on 21 June 1910 in a rural household in Smolensk province, Tvardovsky had an affection and empathy for the overwhelming peasant *narod* [1] that persisted throughout his life. His heroes were simple folk and his poetic language was often the rural idiom that he had heard as a youth and which continued to mark the speech of millions of newly arrived city dwellers.

Yet for all his identification with the peasantry, Tvardovsky no less strongly associated himself with the Soviet régime. He had been only seven years old when the Bolsheviks triumphed, and in his eyes, they were an unquestionably progressive force, bringing literacy and modernization to the backward countryside. Equally important was the fact that the new régime had opened up a world of opportunities for Tvardovsky and his contemporaries that would never have existed without the revolution. Tvardovsky was aware of his position as a favored member of society, but he was also conscious of the fact that he was only one extraordinarily successful representative of a generation that occupied positions which would have been otherwise unattainable. Despite the suffering, the hardships, the fear and repression, these two perceptions evoked in Tvardovsky an enduring, if ultimately anguished, loyalty to the state and to the Communist Party.

His commitment to the Party was put to an agonizing test in 1929 when he chose to denounce his father, a victim of de-kulakization.[2] During all the harsh years of collectivization, moreover, a process that he himself witnessed, his support for the Party, which he joined in 1936, never wavered. His military service during the 1939 campaigns in eastern Poland and Finland only seemed to increase and fortify his enthusiasm. On 20 October, 1939, he wrote to his friend Mikhail Isakovsky, "I've grown to love the Red Army as I formerly loved only the countryside, the *kolkhozy* [collective farms]."[3] Yet although fortunate enough to avoid active duty by virtue of his assignment as a military correspondent, Tvardovsky was mentally and physically exhausted when the war finally ended six years later. In addition to the personal debilitation from which he suffered at the war's conclusion, Tvardovsky was troubled by a sense of unfulfilled expectations. Postwar recovery progressed slowly, or seemingly not at all, and Tvardovsky acutely felt a dichotomy between the promises of the 1930s and the reality of the present.

Tvardovsky's personal crisis lasted into the early 1950s, and it left its mark on early drafts of his poem *Tyorkin na tom svete* (*Tyorkin in the Other World*), about which more will be said later. More importantly, it is the first sign we have of any really deep disaffection with the government and society as they were then structured. It was as yet a rather formless sense of dissatisfaction, one not directed at any particular institution or personality in the Party or government. Tvardovsky felt that something was wrong, but he had not yet labeled the source of his disaffection, be it "cult of personality" or a lack of "truth to life" (*zhiznennaya pravda*) in art.[4]

It was in this state of mind that Alexander Tvardovsky assumed the duties of editor-in-chief of *Novy Mir.*

The 1950s

Prompted perhaps by his doubts, and despite the dangers involved, Tvardovsky made his first cautious steps away from the Party's narrow ideological path while Stalin was still alive. In 1952 he published articles and sketches by Vladimir Tendryakov and Valentin Ovechkin (who was incarcerated in a mental hospital in 1963) that criticized the quality of life in the Russian countryside. Fortunately for Tvardovsky, these pieces were kept away from Stalin, perhaps for fear of angering him.[5] Following Stalin's death on 5 March 1953, several more hesitant moves were made in the direction of increased liberalization in the literary-political arena. In December 1953 Soviet intellectuals were shocked by the appearance of Vladimir

Pomerantsev's article "On Sincerity in Literature,"
which appeared in *Novy Mir*. The publication of this essay is now considered to be a turning point that marked the beginning of the first phase of the "thaw" after Stalin's death. In his article Pomerantsev obliquely criticized the literature of the Stalinist period:

Sincerity—that is what is lacking in some books and plays . . . . Writers not only can but must cast off all devices, tricks and methods for avoiding contradictory and difficult questions . . . . Genuine conflict must be introduced into novels . . . in a year or two you [the reader] will get genuine art.[6]

The appearance of such openly stated opinions on the nature and function of literature caused a furor in the Soviet Union, and both Pomerantsev and *Novy Mir* were severely criticized.

Although the publication of Pomerantsev's article was a daring enough move in itself, Tvardovsky's position was rendered even less secure by the unofficial circulation of his poem *Tyorkin in the Other World*. In this sequel to *Vasily Tyorkin*, the hero, killed in battle, is taken to a Communist underworld which, Tvardovsky makes clear, is a not unrecognizable caricature of Soviet reality. He relentlessly satirizes the monolithic bureaucracy that repeatedly fails to provide for Tyorkin's simplest needs and castigates the attitudes that underlie it:

The dead man admits his mistakes
And, of course, he's lying through his teeth at the same
    time.[7]

Tvardovsky even allows himself a slam at the state censorship organ *(Glavlit)*, describing how the bureaucrat in the underworld *Glavlit* scans the daily newspaper from top to bottom and from bottom to top. The poet also takes some potshots at the official doctrine of class struggle and even goes so far as to allude to some of the most notorious Siberian labor camps by name:

. . . there—through the years
In unseen operation existed
Kolyma and Magadan,
Vorkuta and Narym.[8]

Daring as these criticisms were, they were nevertheless included in the final version of the poem published in 1963. The typescript version which circulated unofficially in 1953–4 was reportedly even more bitingly sarcastic and gloomy.[9]

The final factor which eventually led to Tvardovsky's removal from *Novy Mir* on 17 August 1954 was alcoholism. According to some accounts, Tvardovsky's drinking problem dated back to the war years.[10] We have it on Vladimir Lakshin's authority (at second hand through Solzhenitsyn) that but for his affliction, the editor might not have been removed.

According to Solzhenitsyn, a special meeting of the Central Committee was called to discuss what actions, if any, should be taken to correct *Novy Mir's* ideological "mistakes." It was imperative that Tvardovsky appear at this meeting in a presentable condition, and to this end Samuil Marshak, the noted poet, translator and critic, was "appointed" to watch over him. Tvardovsky, however, managed to slip away from Marshak and got so drunk that he was unable to appear before the Central Committee. There it was decided that since the editor-in-chief could not even manage to turn up at the Central Committee to defend himself and his journal, Tvardovsky had to go.[11] Konstantin Simonov, a well known writer, who had been on the editorial board and who was inclined to continue the efforts to expand the limits of what was permissible in Soviet literature, was chosen to be Tvardovsky's successor. The fact that Tvardovsky was not replaced by a hardline conservative tends to support the Solzhenitsyn-Lakshin account, which portrays both the Central Committee and Khrushchev as not wanting to "persecute" the journal.[12] Instead, they decided to limit the reorganization of the editorial board to the removal of the editor-in-chief. Paradoxically enough, the fact that (according to this version) Tvardovsky was removed for "personal reasons" may thus have helped to preserve the gradual liberalizing process that was taking place in the Soviet literary world and *Novy Mir* in particular.

An official explanation for the turnover at *Novy Mir* appeared on 17 August in *Literaturnaya Gazeta (Literary Gazette)*. *Novy Mir* was severely criticized for providing a forum for the "nihilistic views" on literature expressed by a number of critics, including Pomerantsev, Fyodor Abramov, Mikhail Lifshits, and M. Shcheglov. Their attitudes, it was stated, harkened back to the positions held by some groups of the 1920s and 1930s (especially *Pereval*), which had proven to be incompatible with the Party's prescription for socialist realism. The Writers' Union itself was called to task for not having more effectively monitored the journal, but ultimately the responsibility and blame fell squarely on the editor-in-chief, Tvardovsky.

In his statement before the executive praesidium of the Writers' Union, Tvardovsky claimed that he had been personally and solely responsible for publishing the articles, often over the objections of members of his staff. He refused to give the executive praesidium the satisfaction of hearing him implicate others, as the article in *Literaturnaya Gazeta* noted:

> It is impossible not to note the fact that by taking all blame upon himself, A. Tvardovsky did not say a word about the weight and influence that I. Sats, the former head of the department of criticism, and even M. Lifshits, a supernumerary but permanent consultant of that department, exercised in the editorial office. Later on, other speakers in the discussion named them and correctly evaluated their activity.[13]

It was indeed a dignified performance by the deposed editor-in-chief.

During the four years between his dismissal in 1954 and his reappointment to the chief editorship of *Novy Mir* in 1958, Tvardovsky was occupied mainly by work on his poem *Za dal'yu–dal'* (*Distance beyond Distance*), and by trips to Siberia and abroad. Interestingly enough, although we have seen a sizeable amount of evidence indicating that Tvardovsky's political beliefs had undergone significant change, he appears to have clung stubbornly to his faith in Stalin, perhaps until 1956. On the first anniversary of the dictator's death, hardly a word commemorating him appeared in the Soviet press. One of the very few things that was published in his memory was a canto from *Distance beyond Distance*, a work which appeared in piecemeal fashion throughout the 1950s. This canto, which was not published in later complete editions of the poem, eulogized the dead ruler and made it clear that Tvardovsky had not yet abandoned his faith in him.[14]

In one sense Tvardovsky's reluctance to renounce Stalin during the prolonged period of his active rethinking of his own beliefs is not as contradictory as it may at first appear. To understand the subtle power that Stalin had over individuals, even after his death, one must remember the degree to which all aspects of life in the Soviet Union were politicized. Many people, moreover (especially of Tvardovsky's generation, as has already been mentioned), owed their personal success to the advent of Soviet power, which for twenty-five years had been intrinsically linked with Stalin. Knowing what we do about the horrors of Stalinism, we find it hard to believe that any human being with an ounce of decency could have been a sincere believer in Stalin. Yet there were such Stalinists, and to give up their faith in the supreme leader was an extremely traumatic experience for them.

We do not know precisely when this change occurred in Tvardovsky, although it is extremely unlikely that any loyalty to Stalin remained after Khrushchev's "secret speech" in which he denounced Stalin to the Twentieth Party Congress in 1956. Khrushchev's denunciation of Stalin's "crimes against the Party" in a speech that outlined the policy on which Khrushchev himself was to stake his claim to power, made a profound impression on Tvardovsky. An epoch of official destalinization had begun, and the once-fervent Stalinist Tvardovsky now found himself in agreement with these new political aims.

During the years following the Twentieth Party Congress, the relationship between the party and ideology was significantly, if subtly, altered. Khrushchev's recital of the mistakes that the Party had been led to make by Stalin eroded the Party's claim to be an infallible guide where ideological matters were concerned. Thus, in a sense, the course outlined by Khrushchev in 1956 continued a process begun in

1948 when Tito began to develop a new national brand of Marxism-Leninism which was at odds with Moscow's own. After Stalin's death a gradual change had begun, which did not immediately affect the basic makeup and structure of society, but which concerned the perception and meaning of ideology. Although for people like Tvardovsky the Party retained a guiding role in ideological matters, the individual was now somewhat freer (within certain limits) to make up his own mind. For Tvardovsky, for instance, the ultimate criterion for judging the merit of a literary work became its "truth to life." In assessing its suitability for publication, another criterion had to be added: the degree of danger that it presented to Soviet society and government. Of course there were many who fought bitterly against this liberalizing process. Conservatives and liberals engaged in a tug-of-war contest that reached its most intense levels during Khrushchev's régime but also continued after his removal in 1964.

Ironically enough, it was Tvardovsky's own poem, *Distance beyond Distance,* that contained the first direct literary denunciation of Stalin to appear in print in the Soviet Union. The work, which is structured around the thoughts and observations of a traveler to Siberia and the Far East, offers the reader a rare look at Tvardovsky's inner world during the decade of the 1950s. As early as 1947, when he made his first trip across the Urals, Siberia had assumed a profoundly symbolic meaning for Tvardovsky. He had been overwhelmed by its grandeur, its beauty, and by the significance that this immensely rich region had for the Soviet Union's economic future. Siberia, so huge and unspoiled, was something that he could have faith in, on which he could rest his hopes. During the 1950s,

Tvardovsky attempted to express these feelings in the cantos of *Distance beyond Distance* which appeared periodically in the Soviet press.

The poem opens with an oblique reference to the author's own suffering in the immediate post-war years and contains the canto for which it is best known in the West, "Kak eto bylo" ("How it was"). "Kak eto bylo," published in 1960, deals frankly with the subject of Stalinism:

That was a father whose mere word,
The faintest hint of movement of his brows—
Became law.
Fulfil your harsh duty—
And say that what isn't so,
Is . . .[15]

and earlier:

And those who accompanied him at first,
The underground and prison later knew,
And they took power and struggled,
And disappeared one by one into the shadows.[16]

Tvardovsky also demonstrates a high degree of self-awareness about his own past:

And we [the youth of the 1930s] knew during the
    difficulties of the campaign,
That we were true to the campaign,
That we were true to the banner.
Not we alone,
But the flower of the people
But the honor and the intelligence of the whole coun-
    try.[17]

Still, he later refused to absolve himself and his generation for the crimes and misdeeds of the past:

No, we are a different sort—
Yesterday has not become unknown and unfamiliar to
   us.
We know both these years and the past
And belong to both equally . . .[18] [my italics]

Za dal'yu–dal', encompassing both eulogies of Stalin
and bitter criticisms of his crimes, thus offers us unique
insight into Tvardovsky's development within the
boundaries of what could be published in the Soviet
Union at that time.

Tvardovsky was reappointed editor-in-chief of *Novy
Mir* in June 1958, after the uproar that followed the
appearance in the journal of Dudintsev's novel, *Ne
khlebom edinym (Not by Bread Alone)*. As the 1950s drew
to a close, his time was increasingly taken up by his
editorial and administrative responsibilities. With the
exception of the rather long (but by no means book-
length) poem *Po pravu pamyati (By Right of Memory)*, he
produced only a few dozen lyric poems during his second stint at *Novy Mir*. Instead he became a spokesman
for the interests of a new generation of poets and
writers.

Stylistically, Tvardovsky had little in common with
writers of the so-called Soviet avant-garde such as
Yevgeny Yevtushenko, Vasily Aksyonov, and Andrei
Voznesensky, whose works began to be published during the late 1950s and early 1960s. Tvardovsky was a
classically conservative poet who drew much inspiration from the Russian folk tradition. The younger
poets and writers wished to lessen the ideological, aesthetic, formal, and thematic constraints placed on literature without running the risk of being accused of
exhibiting "bourgeois tendencies." Because he disa-

greed with the directions in which they were moving, works by the "avant-gardists" did not often appear in *Novy Mir,* but Tvardovsky consistently supported their efforts to win approval for their idiosyncratic styles and their sometimes controversial topics. His support became all the more meaningful after the editorial board of *Literaturnaya Moskva (Literary Moscow),* the most progressive Soviet journal, was disbanded in 1959. With its reorganization, *Novy Mir* became the leading spokesman for the "liberal" faction that existed among the public and in the Party and government. It retained that distinction until Tvardovsky's own departure eleven years later.

Tvardovsky, however, failed an important test of his commitment to the goal of allowing more controversial works to be published in the Soviet press. The year 1958 saw the resumption of the campaign against Boris Pasternak, who was that year awarded the Nobel Prize for literature. On 24 October 1958 a letter cosigned by Tvardovsky appeared in *Literaturnaya Gazeta;* the letter termed the Nobel award a "political act, inimical to our country and directed at deepening the cold war." [19] The signatories went further and endorsed a letter by Tvardovsky's predecessors in the *Novy Mir* editorial board, published two years earlier during the height of the campaign launched against Pasternak after the appearance of *Doctor Zhivago* in the West. It is unknown what pressures, if any, were brought to bear to cause Tvardovsky to sign that letter, but his signature appeared there, a witness to the limitations that Soviet writers still either accepted or imposed upon themselves.

Tvardovsky had in the meantime apparently been cultivating supporters in the highest echelons of the party. On 2 February 1959, he delivered a speech to the Twenty-first Party Congress. Here he openly stated his belief that Soviet literature should frankly portray Soviet reality. "Literature, as any other art, can confirm only things which are not imposed on life from without but which are its essence and true nature." [20] Later that year he also read a report to the Third Congress of the Soviet Writers' Union in which he emphasized the need for quality in literature.[21] In 1959 he was re-elected to the RSFSR Supreme Soviet. Thus, as the 1950s drew to a close, his Party career was developing in close conjunction with his career as an editor. For the time being this simultaneous development continued without any major problems. The time was not far off, however, when a changing political climate and Tvardovsky's own personal evolution would combine to bring his Party career and his position in the literary world into irreconcilable conflict.

One Day in the Life of Ivan Denisovich

In November 1961, a manuscript was submitted to the prose section of *Novy Mir* by an unknown mathematics teacher from Ryazan'. It had a rather curious appearance: the manuscript had been typed without any margins, on both sides of the paper, as if its author were either a very frugal man or else did not want to be encumbered with a thick wad of paper. Its outward appearance, however, was not the only thing that distinguished this work from the masses of material submitted every month to *Novy Mir*. The editors in the prose section immediately realized that this novella—entitled simply *Shch-854*—was unusual not only because of its literary excellence but also because of the theme that it treated: life in a forced-labor camp. Accordingly, matters had to handled very carefully. The manuscript was retyped, and two weeks later it was included in a sheaf along with several other works that merited the chief editor's special attention—without, however, any mention of its particular significance.

Tvardovsky took the typescripts home and, already settled in bed for the night, he pulled out *Shch-854*. After only a few pages he too was struck by the work's obvious importance. He got up, put on a shirt and tie to show proper respect and sat down at his desk to read the remainder of the novella. The next morning at work he hailed the appearance of a "new classic" [22] and upbraided his staff for having kept the novella from him for such a long time.

Following the Twenty-second Party Congress in October 1961, Alexander Solzhenitsyn had, after much hesitation made the decision to submit *Shch-854* to *Novy Mir*. The Congress had provided a forum of sorts for the liberal-versus-conservative literary debate. Conservatives such as Vserolod Kochetov and Nikolai Gribachyov had criticized writers they viewed as progressive, such as Yevgeny Yevtushenko and Il'ya Ehrenburg. Their attacks were followed by Tvardovsky's spirited defense of the liberal position in a speech to the Congress[23] and by his subsequent election to candidate membership in the Central Committee. On balance, the actions taken at the Twenty-Second Congress, with its open reaffirmation of the policy outlined by Khrushchev in secret in 1956, constituted a major victory for those who favored a relaxation in the Party's control over various aspects of life in the Soviet Union. Solzhenitsyn had thus decided to try to make use of the liberalizing momentum engendered by the Congress and to submit the most innocuous of his already existing manuscripts to *Novy Mir*.

Shch-854, which was later renamed *One Day in the Life of Ivan Denisovich,* was enthusiastically endorsed by the entire *Novy Mir* editorial board in June of 1962. Because of the work's controversial themes, however, plans to publish it were made very carefully. Tvardovsky could not order its publication on his own authority; the Praesidium of the Central Committee of the CPSU would have to approve it first.[24] It now became a question of winning the support of the Praesidium's membership.

To this end Tvardovsky authorized the distribution of typescripts of the novella among certain selected members of the literary intelligentsia—Kornei Chukovsky, Il'ya Ehrenburg, Venjamen Kaverin and Samuil Marshak, among others. These highly respected litterateurs were then encouraged to write letters to the Praesidium recommending that the work be published. These letters were later included in a file of supporting material that *Novy Mir* sent to Khrushchev along with a copy of the novella in late August or early September. Tvardovsky tried to influence the General Secretary more indirectly through his chief advisor on literature, Vladimir Lebedev. Lebedev was also a friend of Tvardovsky and the two had many conversations about *Ivan Denisovich.* Levedev's enthusiastic advocacy of the novella may well have influenced Khrushchev's decision to endorse it.

In early October 1962, Khrushchev distributed twenty-one specially printed copies of *Ivan Denisovich* to his colleagues in the Praesidium. At its next meeting a few days later, he urged them to approve a resolution allowing the work to be published. Certain members of the Praesidium begged off by saying that they had not had enough time to study the book properly. Despite this weak excuse, which reflected a significant amount of latent opposition to Khrushchev's policy of destalinization, at its next meeting the Praesidium unanimously approved the publication of *Ivan Denisovich*. On 20 October, Khrushchev met with Tvardovsky and told him of the Praesidium's decision. In his memoir Solzhenitsyn describes Tvardovsky's reaction to the news:

. . . Alexander Tvardovsky was as happy as a schoolboy, flitting about the room for all his bearlike bulk. "The bird is free! . . . The bird is free! . . . They can't very well hold it back now! It's almost impossible now!" [25]

In only a few years the "bird" would again sit unhappily in its cage, but for the moment Tvardovsky and his allies celebrated their victory. *One Day in the Life of Ivan Denisovich* appeared in the November 1962 issue of *Novy Mir*, almost exactly one year after its submission to the journal.

In the years that followed the publication of *Ivan Denisovich*, the individual fates of Tvardovsky and Solzhenitsyn became inextricably linked. For this reason it seems appropriate at this point to interject a few words about the relationship that existed between the two men, their sometimes acrimonious but nonetheless enduring alliance which continued until Tvardovsky's death. Tvardovsky, it seems, was willing to gamble on Solzhenitsyn's future for several reasons. First of all, the fact that Ivan Denisovich was a peasant-hero endeared him to the editor. Perhaps the most important reason initially, however, was Tvardovsky's elation and pride in having made so great a "discovery." Solzhenitsyn had appeared on the literary scene as a mature writer whose classically conservative style and use of folk-wisdom struck a sympathetic chord in Tvardovsky. The possessiveness that Tvardovsky felt toward Solzhenitsyn, and which so annoyed the latter, seems to have been the result both of Tvardovsky's "Pygmalion complex" [26] and of his belief that he had a right to expect a certain sort of loyalty from Solzhenitsyn in exchange for the very real risks that he ran for his sake. Solzhenitsyn, however, who never thought that *Novy Mir* had gone far enough in the liberal direction, did not feel the special obligation toward Tvardovsky and his journal that the editor thought was due.

As was mentioned earlier, in the years following the Twentieth Party Congress, Tvardovsky had reassessed his standards for judging the quality of a literary work and had decided that its most important characteristic should be its "truth to life." In Solzhenitsyn Tvardovsky now found a person whose works measured up in a new way to this all-important criterion. His works are, for the most part, of undeniable literary quality, and they grapple with some of the Soviet Union's thorniest problems, both past and present.

A final reason for Tvardovsky's unwavering support of Solzhenitsyn may have lain in the former's sense of guilt for his own past, specifically for his denunciation of his father during the period of collectivization. One need only recall the line from his last work, *By Right of Memory*—"At one moment he was my father, then all at once—an enemy" [27]—to get an idea of the anguish he suffered then and the memories which continued to haunt him. Tvardovsky may have thus tried to expiate his own guilt by becoming a patron of this victim of the repression under which his father had also suffered.

For his part, Solzhenitsyn saw Tvardovsky as a basically well-intentioned but weak man, hopelessly com-

promised, in his eyes, by his loyalty to the Party. Solzhenitsyn had his own goals—to expose completely the
nation's Stalinist past through the publication of his
works—and to this end he was willing to take whatever
advantage he could of Tvardovsky's prestige and
influence in top Party circles. Although he never fully
appreciated the support that Tvardovsky gave him or
the editor's anguish over his own increasingly incompatible roles, Solzhenitsyn did have a certain affection
for him. He liked to think of Tvardovsky as a peasant
transplanted to an urban setting and loved everything
in him that he could trace to the editor's rural background: his "peasant core" and "that peculiar natural
dignity with which he met his enemies. . . ." [28] Although often unnecessarily harsh on Tvardovsky, in
his more sober moments Solzhenitsyn reveals a deep
understanding of their relationship:

We were like two mathematical curves, each illustrating its
own equation. They may approximate at certain points,
may meet, may even have a common tangent, a common
derivative, but their archetypal peculiarity will quickly and
inevitably carry them in different directions.[29]

Ivan Denisovich was highly praised during the first three
weeks that followed its publication. The conservative
wing in the Praesidium, however, headed by Mikhail
Suslov and Frol Kozlov, was hardly content to sit idly
by. The first new signs of resistance to Khrushchev's
policies came at the November 1962 plenum of the
Central Committee elected at the Twenty-Second
Party Congress. A speech he read there was met by his
colleagues with a less than enthusiastic response. Following this plenum, the first articles criticizing *Ivan
Denisovich* began to appear. In spite of these disheleten-
ing signs, Tvardovsky decided to go ahead with the

publication of two short stories by Solzhenitsyn—
"Matryona's House" and "An Incident at Krechetovka Station"—in the journal's January 1963 issue.

The pressure on the chief editor intensified during
the spring of that year. A trip to the United States that
Tvardovsky had scheduled for that spring was can-
celed. He was criticized at a meeting of Party leaders
and members of the intelligentsia held in March. The
rumor that he was about to be fired again circulated in
Moscow. Tvardovsky's response to these attacks took
the form of an editorial that appeared in the April issue of *Novy Mir.* Entitled "Za ideinost' i sotsialistichesky realizm" ("For Ideology and Socialist Realism"), the editorial is a political masterpiece, full of
cosmetic diplomatic concessions. ("We regard this
criticism with the utmost seriousness. It will aid our future work. We have no lack of other deficiencies and
mistakes; we are by no means always pleased by the
level of artistic material that appears in the journal.")[30] Yet Tvardovsky never renounced the general
progressive direction in which he sought to lead the
journal. True to his cautious nature, he took care to
buttress his positions with quotations from Lenin,
Khrushchev, and L. I. Ilyichov, the chairman of the
Central Committee's Ideological Commission. Thus
he noted Khrushchev's pronouncement that "formal-
ism" is "one of the forms of bourgeois ideology" [31] and
slyly adopted Ilyichov's revised definition of socialist
realism:

No, the highest criterion of the essence of socialist realism is
the truth of life, however severe it may be, expressed in artistic form from the position of the Communist world-view.[32]

The appearance of this editorial and, more importantly, Kozlov's heart attack that spring, which effec-

tively ended his opposition to Khrushchev's policies, served to strengthen the General Secretary's control over the Party apparatus. The Party's conservative wing was silenced, at least temporarily.

Another of Solzhenitsyn's short stories, "For the Good of the Cause," was published in *Novy Mir* late that spring. Next Tvardovsky scored what he considered to be a major triumph when he managed to get Solzhenitsyn included in the Soviet delegation to a meeting of the European Community of Writers *(Komesko)* held in August 1963 in Leningrad. To his great surprise, however, Solzhenitsyn refused to go; he did not wish to be a mouthpiece for the official literary organizations. It was but one of the first of many instances that revealed the deep personal and ideological differences that existed between the two men.

Tvardovsky, nevertheless, used the forum provided by the convention to restate his criticisms of the traditional understanding of socialist realism. He maintained that novels written in this style, even though perfectly "correct," often failed to move him.[33] Khrushchev must have agreed with this position, for he included Tvardovsky in a group of Soviet writers and foreign correspondents that he invited to his Black Sea resort at Pitsunda immediately after the conference. There, someone took the initiative to read Tvardovsky's *Tyorkin in the Other World* to Khrushchev. In its final version the poem was still quite a daring satire on Soviet life, but Khrushchev took an immediate liking to it. In fact, he was so eager to see it published that he immediately called up his son-in-law Alexei Adzhubei, who was the editor of the government newspaper *Izvestiya,* and ordered him to print it.[34] In the euphoria that followed the poem's publication that autumn, Tvardovsky and the *Novy Mir* editorial board decided to gamble for big stakes; in late 1963 *Novy Mir* nominated *Ivan Denisovich* for the 1964 Lenin Prize.

In the first weeks of 1964, *Ivan Denisovich* was the overwhelming favorite to win the coveted prize. The novel enjoyed enormous popularity. The last few months, moreover, had seen several important victories for the liberals, and Tvardovsky himself was a member of the selection committee. In March, however, the conservatives abandoned their temporary quiescence. Major newspapers began printing many letters criticizing the novella and giving reasons why it should not be awarded the prize.

It was obvious that the selection committee was badly divided at its first meeting that April. Although *Ivan Denisovich* commanded the largest single bloc of votes, these were cast by the committee's non-Russian representatives plus Tvardovsky (a group which, with the exception of Tvardovsky, constituted the committee's least influential members). Matters took an even more serious turn when S. P. Pavlov, the head of the *Komsomol* (Young Communists), accused Solzhenitsyn of having collaborated with the Germans during the war and of having been imprisoned for a criminal, not a political, offense. Although Tvardovsky defended him vigorously, he was hampered by the fact that he lacked the official documents necessary to disprove the charges. When he was finally able to produce these documents, it was too late. Ilyichev had been sent in to advise the committee to choose the Ukrainian novelist O. Honchar's *Tronka (The Sheepbell)*. After several more votes, *Tronka* was selected and Honchar, who was himself a member of the committee, became the Lenin Prize Laureate for 1964.[35]

Ivan Denisovich's defeat, which was announced on 22

April, was a severe blow not only to Tvardovsky and Solzhenitsyn but to Khrushchev as well. Besides undercutting his policy of destalinization, the events of April revealed the limited degree of control that Khrushchev exercised over the Party machinery. It was now obvious that decisions could be made at certain levels in direct opposition to his avowed wishes; consequently, his prestige was significantly diminished.

After the Lenin Prize débâcle, Tvardovsky accepted an invitation to visit Solzhenitsyn at his home in Ryazan'. This was not to be a social visit, however; Solzhenitsyn had called Tvardovsky away from the office to read his latest work, *The First Circle*. Fueled by vodka, coffee, and cigarettes, Tvardovsky stayed up for several days and nights reading the novel. He reacted to it as only a Russian can, living in a country where the appearance of a major literary work is more than a literary event, being invested with deep social, political and personal meaning. Tvardovsky could not promise to publish it immediately, but he placed a copy of it in the *Novy Mir* safe, and during the summer of 1964 the journal announced that a new work by Solzhenitsyn would be forthcoming.

This, as we know, turned out to be wishful thinking. Early in the autumn Solzhenitsyn's *Krokhotki (Miniature Stories)*, which had been circulating in *samizdat*[36] since the spring, were published in the émigré journal Grani. Tvardovsky, understandably enough, was very upset by this turn of events, which he felt could only damage his chances of getting Solzhenitsyn's new novel past the censors. This setback was overshadowed, however, by Khrushchev's removal from power in October 1964.

Khrushchev and Tvardovsky had enjoyed an unusual relationship that in certain respects could be called an alliance. It was also remarkable for its longevity, for a noted Kremlinologist has traced its origins back to the early 1950s.[37] Whatever the case may be, it is clear that in Khrushchev, Tvardovsky had an ally whose interests were closely aligned with his own. It may have been Khrushchev, in fact, who played a decisive role in appointing Tvardovsky to head *Novy Mir* for a second time in 1958[38] and who kept him from being replaced in 1963. The two men, it appears, had more in common than their peasant background. It was reported, for instance, that Khrushchev and Tvardovsky had discussed the Party's position toward censorship and had both concluded that it could be lifted without endangering the stability of the régime.[39] Khrushchev, too, had his own reasons for backing Tvardovsky and his journal. By the mid-1960s *Novy Mir* had attained a kind of liberalizing momentum which he took an interest in preserving since it coincided with his policy of destalinization.[40] For these reasons, the liberals were later to compare his erratic administration favorably with that of the cautious triumvirate of Brezhnev, Kosygin, and Podgorny.

In spite of Khrushchev's removal, Tvardovsky decided to draw up a contract to publish *The First Circle*. In view of the uncertain political climate, it was, of course, impossible to say when the novel would actually appear in print. *Novy Mir* could only wait and hope for an opportune moment.

In January 1965, Tvardovsky chose to take the offensive in an article commemorating *Novy Mir's* fortieth anniversary, entitled "On the Occasion of an Anniversary." Probably only Tvardovsky could have succeeded in getting such a frank article past the censors, for in it he covers a wide range of controversial topics.

He talks about the past:

Along with all literature, *Novy Mir* experienced the destructive action of certain aspects of our life—the lawless repression, the spirit of distrust and suspicion. It is impossible to forget that many talented writers, whose shining achievements have organically entered into shared cultural experience, were eliminated, morally and physically, from the ranks of Soviet literature.[41]

He severely criticizes the literature of the Stalinist era for its distortions of Soviet reality, especially of rural life, and comes out strongly against the falsification and whitewashing of history in the present. Tvardovsky sets forth the goals of the editorial board—first "as far as possible to give the reader a wide view of the ideological, political, and scientific research and disputes in the Western world," [42] and second, to enhance the quality of Soviet literature by printing only the very best available material. He stoutly defends Solzhenitsyn:

The unusual success of the first of [his works] has not made him into, so to speak, the singer only of the prison camp song, *although it is easy to imagine that the material on that subject, which the author treats, would suffice for a whole writing career.*[43] [my italics]

The boldness of such a declaration can hardly be overemphasized. Tvardovsky closes by reaffirming the course he has charted for the journal:

And we ourselves do not intend to shy away from the presentation of difficult questions and truth in our judgments and evaluations. On that we stand.[44]

"On the Occasion of an Anniversary" was probably the closest thing to a credo that Tvardovsky ever wrote. Its appearance that January was one of the last encouraging signs for the liberals. From that point on, their position slowly but inexorably deteriorated.

Early that year Tvardovsky began to be called more and more often by representatives from the Central Committee to discuss the publication abroad of Solzhenitsyn's *Krokhotki*. This not so subtle pressure made him fear even more the consequences of *The First Circle's* circulation in *samizdat*. He was afraid that the novel, too, would escape abroad, thereby eliminating all chances of its being published in the Soviet Union.

Tvardovsky tried to protect his and Solzhenitsyn's position in two ways. First of all, he advised the latter to write something that could get past the censors, anything that would break the two-year silence. Next, he arranged an appointment for him with P. N. Demichev, the Party's secretary for ideological affairs. That meeting, held on 17 July 1965, came off surprisingly well for Solzhenitsyn, and he and Tvardovsky had some reason to think that in Demichev they had found a person who was not completely unsympathetic.

They needed whatever support they could get, for two heavy blows came in rapid succession that September. The first was the arrest of Andrei Sinyavsky and Yuly Daniel for publishing their work abroad under a pseudonym. Matters were made even more difficult for Tvardovsky because Sinyavsky, a critic, was a frequent contributor to *Novy Mir*. The journal had not yet recovered from the shock produced by the arrests when the second blow landed. On 11 September, the KGB simultaneously raided the apartments of V. L. Teush and I. Zil'berberg, both of whom had a secret "archive" of Solzhenitsyn's work.[45] The agents were rewarded by several copies of *The First Circle,* some verse Solzhenitsyn had composed while still in a labor camp, and most important of all, a copy of *Feast of the Victors.* This was a poem written while Solzhenitsyn languished in prison, so bitter and grim that he himself had renounced it, and it was to be an invaluable tool for the KGB in their campaign against Solzhenitsyn. They brought it up again and again as an example of his latest work, and all of his protestations to the contrary were to no avail.

Solzhenitsyn turned to Tvardovsky for help and advice. The latter, after recovering from his shock and dismay, advised him not to tell anyone that the novel had been taken and to rely on actions behind the scenes to rectify the situation. Solzhenitsyn, however, chose to respond by writing a letter protesting the illegal search and seizure to four Central Committee secretaries, including Demichev. He also tried to persuade Tvardovsky to print a letter by him in which he would answer all the criticisms and refute all the slanderous accusations, one by one. Tvardovsky, however, was furious when he heard about Solzhenitsyn's letter to the Party secretaries. He considered it extremely unwise and counterproductive that Solzhenitsyn had written to four of them instead of addressing himself solely to Demichev, who was more likely than the others to be sympathetic to his requests. At this point Tvardovsky certainly did not feel that he was in a position to publish a letter by Solzhenitsyn—which in any case would not have been passed by the censors. Instead, he renewed his proposal that Solzhenitsyn produce something "acceptable" for the journal, and he himself tried to persuade Demichev to take some action. Neither his contacts in the Central Committee nor the personal relationship that he had tried to cultivate with Kosygin[46] produced any results.

After a promising start, 1966 turned out to hold even more reverses in store for Tvardovsky. He had managed to include Solzhenitsyn's "Zakhar-the-Pouch" in *Novy Mir*'s January issue. The short story had followed an article on the development of the Russian language that Solzhenitsyn had published in the late autumn of 1965 in *Literaturnaya Gazeta*. Any hopes that were raised by these two events proved, however, to be false ones. In March Tvardovsky suffered a crucial setback when he was not re-elected to the Central Committee at the Twenty-third Party Congress. With the loss of his seat in that organization, Tvardovsky lost an invaluable network of contacts and saw his prestige diminish significantly.

Relations between Tvardovsky and Solzhenitsyn, moreover, also deteriorated during this period. That spring the two men quarreled in Tvardovsky's office. Solzhenitsyn felt that Tvardovsky was too possessive, and the latter, conversely, resented the writer's "ingratitude." [47] Tvardovsky criticized him again for having allowed *Krokhotki* to circulate in *samizdat* and for having written the letter to the four Party secretaries. In his memoir Solzhenitsyn gives us this obviously quite biased, but still revealing description of the incident:

All the same, this hard-hitting discussion grew so heated, and A. T. so exasperated by my obstinate disagreement with him at all points, that he jumped up and shouted angrily: "If you piss in his eye he'll say it's dew from Heaven!"

I had done my best to remember all along that he was an erring and enfeebled creature. But now I lost my self-control and answered angrily myself: "Don't try to insult me! I've heard ruder things than that from my former *overseers!*" He made a helpless gesture: "Well, if that's how it is . . ." We were within an inch of a personal quarrel. That would have been quite pointless; it would only have obscured the picture that mattered—that of the schism between two literatures. But none of those present (except, I suppose, Dement'ev) wanted an explosion, and they hastened to prevent it.[48]

After Solzhenitsyn's angry departure, eight months passed before the two men saw each other again.

Tvardovsky left the next day for Italy, but when he returned, the overall situation had not improved. The Political Directorate of the Soviet Army issued a directive forbidding military libraries and army officers to subscribe to *Novy Mir*. This action resulted from the journal's publication of Alexander Makarov's *Home* and Boris Mozhaiev's *From the Life of Fyodor Kuzkin*, works which the Directorate felt gave an uncomplimentary picture of the ordinary Soviet soldier. The order was not rescinded until after Tvardovsky left *Novy Mir* in 1970.

In spite of Tvardovsky's quarrel with Solzhenitsyn and this latest setback, the first discussions about the possibility of publishing Solzhenitsyn's still unfinished novel, *Cancer Ward*, took place in the *Novy Mir* office on 18 June 1966. *The First Circle* had long since been abandoned after the KGB's seizure of the novel, and now the journal's staff was divided on the question of whether *Novy Mir* should push for *Cancer Ward*'s publication. The lower-echelon staff members were strongly in favor of an attempt to print the novel, but the editorial board was just as strongly opposed. After some hesitation, Tvardovsky decided in favor of the publication.

One month later, rumors that *Cancer Ward* had begun to circulate in *samizdat* reached Tvardovsky. He immediately concluded that someone on his own staff must have released it, never dreaming that Solzhenitsyn could have done such a thing after the débâcle that had followed *Krokhotki's* appearance. He wrote to Solzhenitsyn, whom he had not seen since their quarrel, requesting him to come to Moscow and asking him if he knew who the source might be. Solzhenitsyn, who realized what Tvardovsky's reaction would be when he told him that he himself was responsible, wrote the editor a letter in which he admitted that he had allowed the novel to circulate. He maintained, however, that he had the right as an author to do what he wished with his own material. Tvardovsky reportedly wept when he read the letter.[49]

In its August issue *Novy Mir* boldly published a defense of Solzhenitsyn in the form of an article by Vladimir Lakshin. In it Lakshin examines and discards the facile, irrelevant, and contradictory objections of many critics to the story, "Matryona's House." He effectively contrasts these negative appraisals with the overwhelmingly favorable response of the journal's readership to the publication of the work. He concludes that the impact of a literary work is the result of the interaction of three forces—the writer, the reader, and the critic; and the critic (and, by implication, those who stand behind him) has played a disproportionately influential role in the literary process.[50] This carefully worded but nonetheless pointed article was to be the last lengthy public statement to appear in the Soviet press in support of Solzhenitsyn.

Natalya Belinkova describes 1967 as the year that saw "the final expiration of all hopes connected with the thaw."[51] The year began badly for Tvardovsky. Without any warning, the Central Committee reorganized the *Novy Mir* editorial board, removing Tvardovsky's closest friend and top lieutenant, Alexander Dement'ev, as well as B. Zaks. Tvardovsky himself had wanted to retire when he learned that Dement'ev and Zaks were to be replaced, but he was persuaded to stay on as editor-in-chief by Party officials who told him that his retirement could be construed as an "anti-Party act." [52]

Tvardovsky had other troubles besides his difficulties at *Novy Mir*. The dramatized version of *Tyorkin in the Other World* was being produced more and more infrequently and a rumor was circulating that it would soon be removed from the stage altogether. Tvardovsky also felt slighted when several famous writers, including Mikhail Sholokhov, Konstantin Fedin, Leonid Leonov, and Pavlo Tychina, were decorated, and he, who was by now generally considered to be the Soviet Union's premier poet, was left out.

On 15 March, Tvardovsky was again forced to defend his journal at a "discussion" held by the Secretariat of the Writers' Union. He began by repeating his aversion to all forms of "modernism" that were the result of "Western influence." [53] Next, he answered the charge, often leveled at *Novy Mir,* that the journal was somehow suspect because it was praised in the West by noting the international acclaim accorded Shostakovich, Sholokhov, and the Moisseyev dance ensemble. Tvardovsky then took the offensive with a spirited defense of Solzhenitsyn, whose works, he maintained, had influenced some of the best young Soviet writers.[54] Perhaps his most startling pronouncement was his description of censorship as an "archaic organ of our literature." [55] The meeting ended on a surprisingly positive note, with the members of the Secretariat recognizing Tvardovsky as a true "Communist writer" and acknowledging that his journal never printed "tendentious criticisms." [56]

It was fortunate that Tvardovsky and Solzhenitsyn met and put their quarrel behind them on the day following Tvardovsky's minor victory at the Writer's Union Secretariat. For they soon needed to present a united front to the sharp criticism that followed Solzhenitsyn's "Open Letter" to the Fourth Congress of the Soviet Writers' Union in May 1967.

In the autumn of 1966, Solzhenitsyn had decided to abandon his policy of not responding to attacks and began to defend himself openly at lectures and meetings held in schools and institutes. Now he was determined to take advantage of the forum provided by the Writers' Union Congress to air his grievances. In his letter, which he distributed among all the delegates to the Congress, he traced the development of the Party's restrictive, even repressive, role in the nation's literary life and repeated his long-standing complaints: why was *The First Circle* still being held and clandestinely circulated by the KGB? When was some one going to take notice of his disavowal of *Feast of the Victors?* Why had no edition of his collected works been issued? The letter, which soon appeared in the Western press, aroused mixed reactions among the delegates. Many who professed their sympathy with Solzhenitsyn disapproved of his tactics. But to Solzhenitsyn's surprise, Tvardovsky, although he had some reservations about the form of the writer's protest, on the whole reacted favorably to the letter.[57]

Less than a month later, in fact, on 12 June, Tvardovsky declared that *Novy Mir* was ready to publish *Cancer Ward* as soon as he received the necessary authorization. He felt a sense of urgency born of his fear that the appearance abroad of either *Cancer Ward* or *The First Circle* would forestall its publication in the

Soviet Union. Accordingly, he began to push harder and harder for permission to print it as soon as possible.

Tvardovsky also seems to have become more and more open in asserting the independence of his opinions. On 30 June he was called in by a certain Shaur of the Central Committee's cultural section to discuss *Cancer Ward.* At the meeting Shaur tried to persuade Tvardovsky to read *The Feast of the Victors.* Tvardovsky, however, refused even to touch it, calling it a "stolen work," and used language so strong that, as he later told Solzhenitsyn, he could not meet with Shaur again.[58] The May issue of *Yunost'*, moreover, had published two poems by Tvardovsky which gave an only slightly veiled expression of his sentiments:

I myself seek out and admit
All of my shortcomings.
I know them all by heart—
Not by prepared notes. . . .

Only don't crush my spirit,
Don't breathe down my neck.[59]

and

  . . . with great delight,
With wonderful ill-will
All kinds of grey wolves are eating me.

They're eating, but I'm not so green as I look,
For I'm far from being eaten up completely.[60]

These poems clearly reflect Tvardovsky's new sense of *personal* betrayal.

On 22 September, the Writers' Union Secretariat summoned Solzhenitsyn to appear before it to explain the circumstances surrounding his distribution of the

"Open Letter" back in May. Tvardovsky, who was also present, defended him vigorously. Although he acknowledged that he, too, disapproved of the *form* that Solzhenitsyn's protest had taken, he maintained that his complaints were not groundless. In particular Tvardovsky insisted on the obligation of the Writers' Union to refute publicly all the slanderous stories that had been circulated about Solzhenitsyn's past and again pressed the Secretariat for permission to publish *Cancer Ward*. Members of the Secretariat, however, repeated their criticisms of the novel; one warned that its publication would be "worse than Svetlana [Allilueva]'s memoirs." [61] *The Feast of the Victors* was also brought up again and again, along with the demands that Solzhenitsyn publish an "explanation" of his actions and a denunciation of the West. After a statement by him had appeared, then perhaps the Writers' Union would see to his complaints.

The meeting ended on an inconclusive note; neither side was able to claim a victory, for if Solzhenitsyn had not obtained the redress of his grievances that he had sought, neither had the Secretariat been able to wring from him any concessions. Shortly thereafter, Tvardovsky wrote to Solzhenitsyn: "The practical conclusion I draw is that we are prepared to sign a contract with you [to publish *Cancer Ward*] and see what happens." [62] A few days later, Sholokhov rumbled ominously that Solzhenitsyn should be banned entirely. Unfortunately for Tvardovsky and Solzhenitsyn, this likelihood was becoming only too clear.

On 18 December Tvardovsky's spirits were lifted by the news that "someone" was willing to allow *Cancer Ward*'s publication. [63] Several days later Tvardovsky met with K. Voronkov, the General Secretary of the

Writers' Union, who told him that the Union's Secretariat would not oppose the novel's publication. Tvardovsky was ecstatic; he immediately gave the order to have *Cancer Ward* set in type. But the winds shifted again. Tvardovsky was called in for a meeting with the chairman of the Writers' Union Secretariat, Konstantin Fedin, and two of his top aides, Markov and Voronkov, soon after New Year's Day 1968. Fedin, whose tone Tvardovsky later described as "petulant," "embarrassed," and "discontented with himself and all of us," told the editor that the novel's publication would be held up until Solzhenitsyn wrote his "explanation." This, of course, Solzhenitsyn would never do, and thus *Cancer Ward*'s publication was effectively thwarted.[64]

After this blow Tvardovsky immediately sent word for Solzhenitsyn to come to Moscow at once. Solzhenitsyn, however, who displayed a curious indifference to the whole course of events,[65] refused to leave his hideaway in Rozhdevsto. Tvardovsky, for his part, protested against Fedin's decision by means of a strongly worded letter to him on 7 January which the editor delivered to the Secretariat himself. The letter, which later circulated widely in *samizdat,* contained yet another defense of Solzhenitsyn, not just of the writer himself, but also of the progressive trend he then represented:

What matters and is very urgent now is to understand that he is not at the center of attention just as himself—but because, owing to the complicated circumstances [*sic*], he stands at the crossroads of two opposite trends in our literature—one backward-looking, the other forward-looking and keeping with the irreversible movement of history.[66]

Tvardovsky also criticized the pressure that was being placed on Solzhenitsyn to write a statement attacking the West:

> To start with, your insistent demand that Solzhenitsyn should "express his attitude to the West," "give a rebuff," etc., as an absolute condition of surviving as a writer and a citizen, comes strangely from you, because it points in *that* direction, it belongs to practices long since rejected and condemned: "Confess!" "Disassociate yourself from!" "Sign!" Such "confessions" and "rebuffs" as those recently printed in *Literaturnaya Gazeta* [*sic*] over the signature [*sic*] of G. Serebryakova, A. Voznesensky and others do us enormous harm, because they create the image of writers who are morally undiscriminating, lacking in personal dignity and entirely at the mercy of "directives" or "demands"—which, incidentally, are one and the same thing. Do you really think that such confessions serve the interests of the Writers' Union, that they strengthen its authority? I cannot believe it.[67]

Tvardovsky's pleas to Fedin to reconsider his decision were in vain, however. The order had already come down: no more mention of Solzhenitsyn was to be allowed in Soviet publications. Even before Tvardovsky wrote to Fedin, he had had a telephone call from the state publishing house, Goslitizdat, about a reference; the volume was not published until 1971 when the poet lay on his deathbed.

A cable from the émigré journal *Grani* put an end to the *Cancer Ward* affair on 8 April:

> Inform you Committee of State Security via Victor Louis has sent West one more copy *Cancer Ward* to block its publication in *Novy Mir* stop We have therefore decided publish this work immediately.[68]

Tvardovsky's growing sense of "apartness" from the course set down by the Party was heightened by events late that summer in Prague. In the aftermath of the occupation of that city by Warsaw Pact troops on 21 August, the Secretariat of the Writers' Union asked Tvardovsky to cosign a letter to the Czechoslovak Writers' Union, criticizing the Czech writers for supporting "counterrevolutionaries." He refused. Tvardovsky's stand led to a week's delay in printing the letter; when the Union's Secretariat demanded an explanation, he replied that the invasion had precluded his signing any such letter.[69]

Party meetings were ordered and held in all government factories, offices, and institutions to collect signatures for statements expressing support for the invasion. It took two warnings from the District Party Committee before such a meeting was held at *Novy Mir*. Even then Tvardovsky did not attend. Despite his absence there was still some opposition to signing the statement, and at least one party member had to be sent home to achieve the required unanimity.[70]

Tvardovsky began his last major poem, *By Right of Memory*, in the days following the August invasion.[71] In this final work he gives full vent to the hurt and bitterness he felt because of his father's exile. Tvardovsky does not confine himself to expressing his own anguish, but talks of the fate of others, who, after returning from prisoner-of-war camps in Germany, were clapped into labor camps in the Soviet Union:

And after suffering that Christian passion
Half-dead, yet alive—
From one captivity to another—to the boom of victory
    salutes . . .[72]

He denounces the cult that Stalin fostered and warns
    of its resurrection:

So you are already calling for Stalin—
He was a god,
He could return.

And, to the fact that he is forever waiting in the wings
On this earth, of god, a father,
Bears witness now
His Chinese image.[73]

Tvardovsky also succeeded in publishing a short lyrical poem which contained an indirect but clear reference to the events that took place late that August. Describing the autumn weather, he writes:

Windless, warm days—almost hot,
Each one shorter than the last,
The leaves like gold rustle, almost inaudibly
In Moscow itself, in the outskirts of the city,
And somewhere, no doubt, in a park in Prague.[74]

Tvardovsky was clearly moving farther and farther away from an "acceptable" position. Solzhenitsyn tells us that in 1968 the poet began for the first time to listen to foreign broadcasts regularly and to keep up with *samizdat* literature.[75] But there was always a price to be paid. Late that autumn he was one of several nominees to fill a vacancy in the Soviet Academy of Sciences. Because of pressure "from above," however, he was not chosen.[76] On 11 December Tvardovsky sent Solzhenitsyn a telegram wishing him a happy fiftieth birthday: "May you live another fifty years and may your talent lose none of its splendid strength. All else passes; only the truth will remain." [77]

In spite of Tvardovsky's absence from work for much of February and March because of a broken leg, during 1969 *Novy Mir* continued to print works of high literary caliber that were at the same time critical of

certain aspects of Soviet life. On 26 July, for example,
Novy Mir's conservative rival, the journal *Ogonyok*, printed a diatribe entitled "What is *Novy Mir* Against?" It accused *Novy Mir* of publishing:

. . . blasphemous material calling into question the heroic past of our people and of the Soviet Army . . . The articles of criticism purposefully cultivate the tendency to take a sceptical view of the social and moral values of Soviet society, of its ideals, and its achievements.[78]

Tvardovsky tried repeatedly and unsuccessfully to get his recently rewritten version of *By Right of Memory* past the censor. But even though those "at the top" refused to discuss its chances for publication, Tvardovsky did live to see an earlier version of this poem in print. This was no cause for celebration, however. In October Tvardovsky was told that his poem had appeared in the émigré journal *Posev*. He, of course, was extremely upset by this news, which he knew would only be used against him. He immediately rushed off a letter to *Literaturnaya Gazeta* in which he disavowed all responsibility for the poem's publication and denounced "the effrontery of this act, having the intention of discrediting my work." [79] The editors of *Literaturnaya Gazeta,* however, chose not to print Tvardovsky's letter immediately.

This blow was soon followed by Solzhenitsyn's expulsion from the Ryazan' branch of the Writers' Union on 4 November and from the RSFSR Writers' Union the next day. Solzhenitsyn responded by writing an angry letter to the RSFSR Writers' Union Secretariat. In general, however, the reaction of the Soviet intelligentsia was rather muted, although Zhores Medvedev tells us that there were rumors to the effect that Tvardovsky had led a group of writers to demand that the USSR Writers' Union Secretariat be called to meet in an extraordinary session to revoke the action taken by the RSFSR Union.[80] However apocryphal that story may be, we do know that Tvardovsky was upset by Solzhenitsyn's letter. Solzhenitsyn's visit to his office on 11 November ended in another stormy scene.

With Solzhenitsyn's expulsion Tvardovsky understood that it was only a matter of time before he and his journal were also struck down. Indeed, by the end of 1969, Voronkov was offering Tvardovsky a chance to exit gracefully. Tvardovsky had an *ex officio* seat in the Writers' Union Secretariat; it was now suggested that he leave *Novy Mir* and take the position of full-time staff secretary, with its higher salary and greater Party status. Tvardovsky, however, refused to be kicked upstairs.

Yet for all his outward show of resolution in the face of unrelenting pressure, Tvardovsky had grown jaded and despondent. In a letter dated 3 November 1969, he wrote to Isakovsy:

My life at the dacha would be completely satisfactory if I didn't unfortunately have to make so many trips to the city to work, where unhappy affairs and exhausting worries always await me. Oh well, the hell with them.[81]

Lakshin, too, recalled that during his last year at *Novy Mir*, Tvardovsky expressed a similar attitude in a poem, probably his own, that he recited:

It is as though our time's grown hollow:
What filled it once has gone,
And even what we hoped would follow
Will never now be done.
The body lives today, tomorrow;
The soul from it is gone.[82]

As 1970 began, the pressure continued to increase.
The critic Yevgeny Ovcharenko denounced Tvardovsky as a "kulak poet" (again!) at a writers'
plenum.[83] Voronkov summoned Tvardovsky to his
office *every day* to discuss the situation and even pressed
him to hire Ovcharenko at *Novy Mir*. Finally it was decided that instead of having the Central Committee
issue a resolution removing Tvardovsky from his post,
an action that seemed too heavy handed to some, the
Writers' Union Secretariat would reorganize the *Novy
Mir* editorial board, thereby forcing Tvardovsky to resign. On 10 February, the decision to remove
Tvardovsky's top men, V. Y. Lakshin, A. I. Kondratovich, and I. Vinogradov, was made; their replace-
ments included some of *Novy Mir's* harshest critics,
among them Ovcharenko. The following day, Alexander Tvardovsky wrote to the Writers' Union Secretariat asking to be relieved of his responsibilities at *Novy
Mir*. On the same day, both an article announcing the
reorganization at *Novy Mir* and Tvardovsky's old letter
about the publication of *By Right of Memory* were
printed in *Literaturnaya Gazeta*. The implication that
the two were connected was clear.

Tvardovsky had to endure at least two weeks in the
gloom of his office before his replacement, V. A. Kosolapov, arrived.[84] When he finally left, he dropped almost completely out of sight. In early June he reap-
peared briefly to come to the aid of Zhores Medvedev,
who had been confined in a mental hospital at the end
of May. As Medvedev later described it:

Throughout this period of detention, Tvardovsky and
Solzhenitsyn, together with many other friends and colleagues, gave me great moral and practical support. When I
came into the visitors' room at the Kaluga psychiatric hospi-

tal on 9 June and saw Alexander Tvardovsky, who embraced me, I found it very difficult to restrain my tears.[85]

According to Medvedev's brother's account of the ordeal in *A Question of Madness*, Tvardovsky played an important role in obtaining Zhores's release in June.

Tvardovsky's sixtieth birthday later that month was widely noted, but in enumerating his contributions to Soviet literature, no one mentioned his work at the head of the country's most influential journal. Instead, the articles dwelt exclusively on his career as a poet.

Near the end of the summer, Tvardovsky's health failed. He suffered a stroke that left him partially paralyzed. While tests were being run on him in the Kremlin Hospital, it was discovered that he had a large cancerous tumor in his lungs, the result of many years of heavy smoking. Recovery was out of the question; Tvardovsky was given only about a month to live.

Tvardovsky was released from the hospital during the autumn of 1970 and was taken to his dacha in Pakhra, outside Moscow. Although his speech was impaired and his right side paralyzed, he understood the significance of the Nobel Prize in literature, awarded to Solzhenitsyn on 8 October. "It's our prize, too," he remarked to Roy Medvedev, having in mind the old *Novy Mir* editorial board.[86]

Tvardovsky's condition slowly deteriorated over the course of the next few months. When Mstislav Rostropovich and Solzhenitsyn went to visit him at his apartment in Moscow that February 1971, they found the poet an almost complete physical ruin. Tvardovsky could utter only an occasional disjointed word, and the paralysis had almost totally immobilized him. Solzhenitsyn left him a copy of his recently finished *August*

1914, never thinking that Tvardovsky would manage to get through even a portion of it.

When Solzhenitsyn returned to see him that May, he was surprised by the improvement in Tvardovsky's condition. Indeed the poet had astounded the doctors by his tenacity. To Solzhenitsyn's amazement, Tvardovsky had read or had listened to the entire novel. "Marvelous," he pronounced.[87]

Tvardovsky was rendered one final honor by the state on Revolution Day (7 November) when he was awarded a State (formerly Stalin) Prize, together with Vadim Kozhevnikov.[88] But he could not go on postponing the inevitable through sheer strength of will. Although he held on through the summer and into the autumn, Tvardovsky's condition necessitated his readmission to the Kremlin Hospital in November. He died there on the night of 18 December 1971.

Tvardovsky's death was met by a restrained official response. As had been the case on his sixtieth birthday, the obituaries stressed his literary production and ignored his years at *Novy Mir.* Solzhenitsyn, however, had the last word in an elegy he composed after the funeral:

There are many ways of killing a poet. The method chosen for Tvardovsky was to take away his offspring, his passion, his journal.

The sixteen years of insults meekly endured by this hero were as nothing so long as his journal survived, so long as literature was not stopped, so long as people could be printed in it, so long as people could go on reading it. But then they heaped the coals of disbandment, destruction and mortification upon him, and within six months these coals had consumed him. Within six months he took to his deathbed, and only his characteristic fortitude sustained him till now, to the last drop of consciousness of suffering.

For the third day now the portrait hangs over the coffin—there the dead man is still only forty, his brow unfurrowed by the sweetly bitter burdens of his journal, radiant with the childishly luminescent trust that he managed to carry with him throughout his mortal life and that returned to him even when already doomed.[89]

Tvardovsky once summed up his feelings on his role as guardian of the quality of literature in a politically and ideologically restrictive environment, the limitations of which he accepted to a certain degree:

I don't think we shall be taken to task in the next world for not having done what we *couldn't* have done; but if we *could* have done something and didn't—for that we will be punished.[90]

Yet if Solzhenitsyn's occasional exploitation of the editor's position and his rash actions ended in his expulsion from the Soviet Union, Tvardovsky's efforts to create a "Communism with a human face" were no more successful. For both men were operating under mistaken assumptions: Solzhenitsyn, believing the régime would allow itself to be forced into an all-out confrontation with him; Tvardovsky, hopeful that the changes inaugurated at the Twentieth Party Congress would be followed through to their logical conclusions. Both men, as it turned out, were wrong, but Tvardovsky's predicament was the more cruel since each defeat shook his faith in the system to the core while setbacks only confirmed Solzhenitsyn in the justice of his cause.

Tvardovsky once exclaimed to Solzhenitsyn:

"How could anyone possibly say that the October Revolution was in vain! . . . But for the Revolution, Isakovsky would never have been discovered! . . . And what would have become of me without the Revolution? . . . "[91]

And here Tvardovsky had not only himself in mind but his entire generation.[92] It was this part of Tvardovsky's character, this bedrock feeling of unity with his generation and with the Soviet *narod*, that Solzhenitsyn could never understand. Drawn in opposite directions by his equally sincere desires to serve the Party that had created the October Revolution and to seek higher levels of truth and quality in literature, Tvardovsky's own inner conflict deepened. Pushed both by Solzhenitsyn's influence and by his own basic sense of decency, he became more and more ideologically isolated from his peers in the Party. He who was at heart an "organization man," a member of the "establishment," found himself excluded in the end. He could find only occasional solace in reflecting that he was heir to the tradition of Nekrasov, the noted nineteenth-century poet and editor who had been subjected to professional pressures and had been a victim of political intrigue and rumor.

Tvardovsky had a singular talent for capturing in his works the spirit of each of the great epochs of Soviet history that he lived through: collectivization, war, reconstruction, destalinization. Indeed, it is in this ability more than in any other that lies his significance as both an artist and as an historical figure. His "peasant" directness and simplicity and his consciousness of himself as a favored representative of the generation and class that benefited from an immense social and economic upheaval combined with his natural artistic talent to produce a poet who was, in a sense, a national chronicler.

Yet Tvardovsky's role was by no means as passive a one as that description might seem to imply. He was, as we have seen, an ardent defender of his artistic and moral convictions, and he became ever more troubled as these convictions began to conflict more and more often with the policy of the Party to which he owed everything. For Tvardovsky there was no way out. Being a basically decent man, he could not turn away from his deeply held beliefs. Yet he was bound to the Party not only by the habit of long-standing loyalty but also by his early recognition of it as the bringer of culture, progress, and opportunity to the backward countryside. It was this dichotomy that was, in the end, the primary source of the anguish he suffered until he died.

Alexander Tvardovsky, 1968

The last meeting of the *Novy Mir* editorial board under Tvardovsky, 1970. Seated, left to right: Zaks, Dement'ev, Tvardovsky, Kondratovich, Maryamov. Standing: Khitrov, Lakshin, Dorosh, Vinogradov, Sats.

The Politics of *Novy Mir* under Tvardovsky

Linda Aldwinckle

The Journalistic Traditions of *Novy Mir*

Novy Mir (New World)—a "literary-artistic and sociopolitical journal," as it is defined on its title page—has its roots in the traditions of the nineteenth-century "thick" journal, a peculiarly Russian phenomenon with no direct analogues in Western Europe or the U.S.A., where the journal has tended to be either academic, catering to a specialist in a particular field, or illustrative, catering for an indeterminate "mass" reader. The main feature of the thick journal is that it embraces fiction, literary criticism, and sociopolitical journalism. Its precursor was the encyclopaedic journal which aimed to enlighten the Russian people by propagating new ideas in many fields of knowledge. The thick journal preserved this educational function but it was also organized to reflect a specific ideology. Probably the most important of these journals in nineteenth-century Russia was *Sovremennik (The Contemporary)*. Originally founded by Puskhin in 1836, the year before his death, the journal's relative lack of success for its first decade is ascribed by some commentators to its exclusively literary character and absence of a political stance. Sold to Nekrasov and Panayev in 1846, *Sovremennik* thereafter adopted as consistently radical a viewpoint as the censor would permit, and became for twenty years the focus of political opposition within the intelligentsia, the country's small but growing educated class. This definite ideological position gave the journal a much increased circulation and great influence as a progressive, democratic, even revolutionary forum.

Literary criticism played a key role in the makeup of the nineteenth-century thick journal. Because of the strict censorship, dissident social and political ideas had to be disguised in artistical form; hence literary criticism was oriented toward the illumination of social rather than aesthetic problems. This was justified by revolutionary democrats not in terms of mere expediency but as a consequence of their belief that because art was a way of thinking in images, it could be the means for the direct contemplation of truth. The critic Belinsky (who was the de facto editor of *Sovremennik* in 1847–8) held that literature was "the vital spring from which all human sentiments and conceptions percolate into society."

After the closure of *Sovremennik's* successor, *Otechestvenniye Zapiski (Notes of the Fatherland)*, the traditions of the thick journal were transferred to the underground Marxist press published outside Russia. The thick journal did not appear again on Russian soil until it was recreated in a journal entitled *Red Virgin Soil* as a deliberate act of Bolshevik policy in 1921, since its fusion of literature and social issues complemented the new régime's Marxist view that the dominant ideology of a particular society was mirrored in all branches of its culture.

Novy Mir was created in 1925 as a forum for writers of all political tendencies, including the fellow-travelers who were excluded from such exclusively leftist journals as *LEF (Left Front,* representing the Left Futurist movement) and *Na Postu (On Guard,* organ of the Russian Association of Proletarian Writers; for brevity, this organization is referred to by its Russian initials as RAPP). Lunacharsky, the first Soviet Commissar of Education, and Steklov were appointed as *Novy Mir's* first editors, but its real guiding force was Vyacheslav Polonsky, who was admitted to the editorial board the following year. In his joint role as editor and critic, Polonsky argued vehemently against the class theory of culture propagated by the proletarian writers. In a major article in *Novy Mir,* "Artists and Classes," [1] he debunked the theory of "social command," [2] claiming that it represented an attempt by the intelligentsia to assume the role of artistic mouthpiece for the working class. Polonsky maintained that one did not have to be an organic part of the proletariat to produce works that reflected the revolution. Each social group made its own contribution to Soviet culture.

In his editorial celebrating the journal's fortieth anniversary,[3] Aleksandr Tvardovsky noted that *Novy Mir* could not be considered to have been a single entity throughout the period of its existence, since this time span included many different stages in the sociopolitical and literary life of the Soviet Union. In the early history of the journal a crucial turning point was the year 1931, in which Lunacharsky and Polonsky were both forced out because of attacks from RAPP. The 1920s was a period of intellectual ferment during which various literary groups competed against each other, although none succeeded in establishing hegemony. The thick journals were the forums for these polemics, which derived from differing interpretations of the function of literature in Soviet society. In October 1931 Stalin intervened, calling a halt to free intellectual debate and demanding stricter application of the notion of *partiinost'* (party-mindedness).[4] This was followed by the Central Committee resolution of 23 April 1932 which dissolved all literary groups, incorporating them into a projected Union of Soviet Writers. This institutionalization of ideological orthodoxy brought about the demise of the thick journal, which had thrived on the strength of its individual critical platform. From 1932 onward the surviving journals were barely distinguishable one from the other. Although *Novy Mir* published a few works of literary quality, this was not enough to endow it with the distinctive character that is essential to the existence of the thick journal. Criticism disappeared from its pages under the editorship of Gronsky (1932–7) and Stavsky (1937–9). During the years of World War II the journals played a secondary role to newspapers. In 1946 Konstantin Simonov became editor of *Novy Mir* but did not turn it in any particular direction. In 1950 he handed over the reins of the journal to Tvardovsky. Thus, prior to Tvardovsky's editorship, *Novy Mir* had flourished as a true thick journal for only six years, from 1925 to 1931. But the principles it fostered during that stage—its opposition to dogmatism and its commitment to a philosophical ideal rather than to political "needs"—were to exert a lasting influence on the journal's physiognomy and to reappear under the editorship of Tvardovsky in the 1960s.

Novy Mir in the 1950s

In the nineteenth century, if a thick journal fell into political disfavor, it was as a rule arbitrarily closed down. A new journal would then spring up, bearing a different name but the same ideological stance as its predecessor. In recent years in the Soviet Union, total shutdown has not normally been employed as a form of ideological suppression.[5] Rather, the chief editor is dismissed, either on direct instructions from the Party Central Committee or at least with its tacit approval. Although there are elements of continuity that survive changes of editorship, to a large degree each new editor constitutes a new journal, since the individual tone of a journal is largely set by its chief editor's personality and political views. At the same time, however, it is also conditioned by the nature of the times in which the editor is obliged to function. When Tvardovsky first took over as chief editor in 1950, there were still three more years of Stalin's rule ahead of him; yet despite certain factors of continuity, the *Novy Mir* of the 1960s, when Tvardovsky was editor for the second time, constituted a different journal from the *Novy Mir* of 1950–4. This was because the political determinants of Soviet cultural life underwent dramatic and far-reaching changes during the latter half of the 1950s. Tvardovsky began his second editorial term in 1958, in the wake of the Twentieth Party Congress (1956) and the ensuing policy of destalinization.

Throughout the 1950s *Novy Mir* cannot be said to have shown the distinctive profile that characterized the traditional thick journal. The only widely acknowledged contribution of Tvardovsky's first term toward creating such a profile was the publication of Valentin Ovechkin's essays entitled "Everyday Life in the Countryside," [6] These initiated a critical approach to the problems of Soviet agriculture, and were the forerunners of perhaps the most important trend in Soviet literature of the 1960s—that of "village prose." This innovative step by Tvardovsky seems, however, to have been an isolated action rather than part of a consistent editorial policy.

Two main factors determine the ideological "line" of a Soviet journal: first, the journal's self-image and conscious aims; second, the reactions to it of outside forces, namely society (in the form of public opinion) and its political leaders (in the form of policy statements and direct executive action). If *Novy Mir* is judged solely in terms of the first factor, then the contention that it did not represent any particular line during the first Tvardovsky period is entirely justified. The editorial board did not enunciate any general guiding principles nor propose any specific goals for the journal. The content of *Novy Mir* as a whole reflected this lack of a stated policy; it contained a mixture of Stalinist dogma and tentative liberalism, and no editorial stamp on the journal could be detected.

With regard to the second factor—the reaction of outside forces to *Novy Mir*—it is impossible as yet to reach a definitive conclusion, since there is a dearth of sociological data in the Soviet Union which reflects public opinion. A feature of the journal in the 1960s, however, was the way in which it encouraged feedback from its readers, thereby promoting the participation of the public in creating the journal's line. The readers became to some extent a "barometer of the social climate," [7] as they had more truly been in the 1840s when the reader's letter was first introduced to the thick journal.

Policy statements by Soviet leaders on matters concerning literature are generally dictated by immediate political concerns. They tend to react publicly to a journal only if they consider that it is at odds with Party policy, whether general or specific. In 1954 direct action was taken against *Novy Mir* in the form of a resolution passed by the Praesidium of the Writers' Union and approved by the Party Central Committee, which attacked the whole tenor of the journal and accused it of following an independent line. This expression of official disapproval was basically pragmatic, occasioned by the unstable political situation after the death of Stalin in which various factions were jockeying for supremacy. By challenging ideological orthodoxy with its publication of V. Pomerantsev's article

"On Sincerity in Literature" in December 1953, *Novy Mir* was supporting a measure of liberalization feared by cautious politicians. Moreover, in early 1954 Tvardovsky submitted the first version of his poem *Tyorkin in the Other World* to the Central Committee for approval. It incurred Party displeasure by its bold anti-Stalinist tone and was, according to Lakshin,[8] the main reason why the Party approved Tvardovsky's dismissal from *Novy Mir* in the autumn of 1954.

In 1958 Tvardovsky regained the editorship of *Novy Mir,* apparently with Khrushchev's approval, after Simonov had overstepped the mark by publishing V. Dudintsev's controversial novel *Not by Bread Alone.* Despite the "thaw" that began in 1956, when in 1958 Tvardovsky took over *Novy Mir* for the second time, it was indistinguishable from other journals. Nor did it show any early signs of change. The period between Tvardovsky's reappointment as editor and the Twenty-second Party Congress in October 1961 was relatively uneventful; it was marked by the Pasternak affair and the Third Congress of Soviet Writers, both of which had a sobering effect on the literary intelligentsia.

The Significance of *One Day in the Life of Ivan Denisovich*

It was after Tvardovsky's speech at the Twenty-second Party Congress calling for bolder material on "phenomena that counteract our advance and that our literature must expose"[9] that Solzhenitsyn decided to send a copy of *One Day in the Life of Ivan Denisovich* to *Novy Mir* through his friend and former fellow-prisoner Lev Kopelev, who was a regular contributor to the journal. An account of the sequence of events leading up to the publication of the novella in November 1962 has been given by Solzhenitsyn in his memoir *The Oak and the Calf*. No one imagined that the story would ever be published without the approval of the Party Praesidium. Solzhenitsyn, however, accuses Tvardovsky of having failed to act with a sense of urgency because he hated to be rebuffed by his political superiors, and that as a result "Literature could have accelerated history. It failed to do so." [10]

In his essay *Solzhenitsyn, Tvardovsky and Novy Mir,* Lakshin maintains that Tvardovsky proceeded with intelligent caution, as one false step could have destroyed all chance of publication. He states that Tvardovsky was not in a position to have gone straight to Khrushchev. Moreover, in his carefully written preface to *Ivan Denisovich,* Tvardovsky was announcing to society that its publication was a conscious step on the part of *Novy Mir* and not an editorial oversight, such as had occurred with the publication of Dudintsev's novel in 1956.

It soon became clear that Khrushchev's destalinization campaign had influential opponents who were determined to make their weight felt. The following month—December 1962—witnessed a wave of reaction that induced a temporary waning of Khrushchev's influence. In fact, the publication of Solzhenitsyn's story could not have served as a political precedent (as Solzhenitsyn claims it might have done) for it was the result of an exceptional action—the direct intervention of the Party Praesidium as a body. There would have been no question of Tvardovsky being able subsequently to turn to Khrushchev to request publication of every ideologically doubtful work, for Khrushchev was never in a position to have personally authorized publication.

The publication of Solzhenitsyn's story did, however, have a decisive moral influence on the development of Soviet literature, for it liberated the reading and writing public from the conspiracy of silence of the Stalin era. It encouraged the hope that other works which truthfully explored the past would also be printed. The process of *samotyok*,[11] of which *One Day in the Life of Ivan Denisovich* was itself a product, swelled enormously as a result of Tvardovsky's deliberate step toward a liberal editorial policy and was a major force in the development of *Novy Mir*'s line. Firstly, it created a writers' *aktiv*[12]—a wide circle of previously unknown, predominantly young writers, who, as a consequence of the publication of Solzhenitsyn's story, identified with the anti-Stalinist platform of *Novy Mir* and sent their main works to it. Its most prominent members included Fyodor Abramov, Vasily Belov, Vasil' Bykov, Efim Dorosh, I. Grekova, Fazil Iskander, V. Likhonosov, Boris Mozhayev, Vassily Shukshin, Alexander Solzhenitsyn, Vitaly Syomin, Georgii Vladimov, and Vladimir Voinovich, as well as such older-established writers as Viktor Nekrasov, Valentin Katayev and Veniamin Kaverin. The commitment of these talented writers to *Novy Mir* provided the journal with essential support. Another vital form of backing came from the readers' *aktiv*—"that powerful, genuinely democratic spearhead of public opinion, without which real literary life cannot exist."[13] This readers' *aktiv* demonstrated its approval by writing letters of encouragement and constructive criticism to the journal.

The third and perhaps most decisive way in which *samotyok* influenced the direction of *Novy Mir* was in its literary criticism, for it was in response to this creative surge from the public that Lakshin, whom Tvardovsky

appointed as chief literary critic in 1963, formulated
the program that underlay *Novy Mir*'s approach to literary criticism. This had a two-fold function: in
sharing its assumptions, writer and reader were linked
by a common basis for the exchange of ideas, and it
provided the journal with a coherent "philosophy."

In his first major article on this subject in *Novy Mir*
Lakshin set out specifically to defend *One Day in the Life
of Ivan Denisovich* from the criticism to which it had
been subjected in 1963.[14] He also, however, moved
from the particular to the general and attacked the
prevailing form of normative criticism with its dogmatic, restrictive conceptions of literature: what the
hero should be like, how much social criticism should
be permitted, and so on. In effect, he was rejecting the
method of "socialist realism" as it had been practiced
since the 1930s. Lakshin advocated in its place an ana-
lytical method based on the aesthetics of the
nineteenth-century radical democrat Dobrolyubov.
This consisted of approaching a work as a reflection of
life and—"proceeding from the testimony of the artist,
pronouncing judgment on the work itself and on the
life portrayed in it."[15] Lakshin thus stated his intention to reintroduce the concept of value judgments
into literary criticism, subjecting works to both an aesthetic and a sociological scrutiny. This approach to
criticism, with a sociological orientation, was to become the essence of *Novy Mir*'s platform in the 1960s.

After attacking the schematic, "quantitative"
method of Solzhenitsyn's critics, Lakshin passed to a
qualitative analysis of the story. In the process he
defined the values underlying his critical judgments:
first and foremost was his belief that truth was embodied in the empirical facts of everyday life and not in
abstract theory. Lakshin also proclaimed his belief in a

democratist view of society; hence the task of literature was to focus on the lives of ordinary people rather than on the feats of Party leaders and government administrators as had happened during Stalin's personality cult. The third value underlying Lakshin's criticism was his respect for the dignity and freedom of the individual personality. His appreciation of Solzhenitsyn's work was based on the way in which the writer constantly linked the physical and moral aspects of man. The moral nature of Ivan Denisovich was not derived from an abstract philosophy, separate from his personality and imposed upon it by the author, but was a "direct attitude to life, to people, and to work." [16] This was also an innovation after the Stalinist "production" novels, in which the inner life of the hero had been totally unconnected with external reality.

These criteria of value, on which Lakshin founded his critical analyses, were the moral essence of *Novy Mir*'s platform in the 1960s. The principles of truthfulness, of democratism, and of the dignity of the individual were primarily ethical criteria and only secondarily sociopolitical, for the former determined the latter. The common ideological ground that gave *Novy Mir* its distinctive physiognomy in the 1960s derived from the practical application of these ethical criteria to a critique of Soviet society.

Lakshin's impressive article, which appeared in *Novy Mir*'s first issue for 1964, was seen as a strong recommendation from the liberal intelligentsia for the award of the Lenin Prize to Solzhenitsyn. The manipulations of the neo-Stalinists to deprive him of the prize are well known, and resulted in damage to *Novy Mir* as well. The journal, however, strengthened its position during 1964 by publishing Sergei Zalygin's *On the Irtysh*,[17] which revealed the arbitrary, bureaucratic methods by which collectivization had been implemented, and Yury Dombrovsky's *The Keeper of Antiquities*,[18] which described the arrest of an innocent man by the secret police in 1933. In August Tvardovsky dramatically announced his intention to publish Solzhenitsyn's *The First Circle*.

During the last few months of Khrushchev's administration the censorship had made life so difficult for Tvardovsky that he believed the position of the journal could only improve under the new collective leadership. In his article on the fortieth anniversary of *Novy Mir*,[19] Tvardovsky enunciated the principles of its editorial policy, already formulated by Lakshin. He refuted the charge leveled at *Novy Mir* that the revelation of the truth about Stalin's personality cult could be exploited by enemies of the Soviet Union; rather he proclaimed that truth by its very nature could be only beneficial. Tvardovsky supported the democratic principle which encouraged literature to focus on the plight of the "little man," in the tradition of Russian nineteenth-century literature, instead of creating an idealized hero as had been the rule under Stalin. He stressed the importance not of the author's ideological orthodoxy but of his individual conscience. "It is the personality [*lichnost'*] of the author that determines the merits of a work as an artistic whole." [20] Tvardovsky concluded by saying that these concepts were those which guided the everyday editorial practice of *Novy Mir*.

During the first half of 1965 *Novy Mir* published the final and most controversial installment of Ilya Ehrenburg's memoirs, and the sequel to Viktor Nekrasov's travel notes on the West, the first part of which had come under heavy fire in 1963. Lakshin contributed an article on the relationship between reader, writer, and critic, in which he called on critics to follow the example of the reading public and reject the dogmas of the past. He stressed his belief that the value of a literary hero could not be based on his conformity to the norms of Party ideology but only on his moral significance for the reader. In June, *Novy Mir* published Vitaly Syomin's "Seven in One House," as if to illustrate its thesis that the heroic did not lie in spectacular feats but in overcoming the constant difficulties of everyday life.

Novy Mir thus strengthened its position as a forum for the liberalizing forces in Soviet society. In September 1965, however, it suffered a double setback. The leadership embarked on a tough policy of attempting to intimidate the liberal intelligentsia. Sinyavsky and Daniel were arrested and charged with anti-Soviet activity, and in the accompanying searches Solzhenitsyn's archive was confiscated. Since both Sinyavsky and Solzhenitsyn were closely associated with *Novy Mir*, Tvardovsky found himself in a particularly exposed and vulnerable position.

Tvardovsky and His Editorial Board

The Twenty-second Party Congress in 1961 had marked the high spot of Tvardovsky's political career, with his election to the Central Committee as a candidate member. When the Twenty-third Congress convened in March 1966, Tvardovsky was not only dropped from candidate membership of the Central Committee but even failed to be elected as a delegate. Solzhenitsyn tried to convince him that this was a liberation from political obligations but Tvardovsky was extremely upset by this blow to his prestige. He was, no doubt, keenly aware that with his loss of political influence *Novy Mir* would become even more subject to ideological constraints.

In the repressive climate of 1966, in which Solzhenitsyn and Daniel were tried and convicted of publishing anti-Soviet works abroad, several works were thrown out of *Novy Mir* by the censorship, including Alexandr Bek's novel *The New Appointment,* which criticized the workings of Soviet bureaucray, and Konstantin Simonov's war diaries. Awareness of the instability of *Novy Mir's* position, induced by these acts of repression from above, brought about a split within the editorial board on the policy of *Novy Mir.* The senior members, Dement'ev and Zaks,[21] wanted to be more cautious and impose an even greater degree of self-restraint. This would have played into the hands of the opponents of *Novy Mir,* who hoped that the journal would voluntarily sacrifice its critical platform for the sake of survival. The junior members—Lakshin, Maryamov, and Vinogradov, supported by their editorial staff—reacted to the danger in completely the opposite fashion. Under threat of extinction, they wanted to fight back with even greater intensity since they valued the defense of the journal's principles above their own material and psychological security. Since they believed that every issue of *Novy Mir* might be the last, they felt they had nothing to lose by struggling to achieve the maximum possible.[22] The split between the upper and lower strata of *Novy Mir* was clearly demonstrated by the decision taken concerning the publication of *Cancer Ward.* Solzhenitsyn offered the first part of the novel to the journal in the spring of 1966. An editorial discussion was held in June in which Lakshin, Vinogradov, Maryamov, and Anna Berzer all spoke in favor of publication. Lakshin and Maryamov said that they regarded their standpoint as a moral duty to the reader. Vinogradov put it succinctly: "If we don't print this, I see no reason for our existence." [23] Dement'ev and Zaks, on the other hand, expressed their fears about the ideological aspect of the novel, but Tvardovsky brushed their reservations aside and came down decisively in favor of the younger faction.

A week later another editorial meeting was held at which Tvardovsky changed his tune, saying that it was too risky to attempt publication of the novel that year. Dement'ev had clearly used his sobering influence over Tvardovsky to dissuade him from such a bold venture. Neither Lakshin nor Maryamov was present at the meeting to counteract the conservative forces which had won over Tvardovsky to their side. The reason given by Tvardovsky was that there was already a blockage of works in the pipeline awaiting the censor's approval, including Bek's novel and Simonov's diaries. Publication was thus deferred indefinitely and Solzhenitsyn removed his manuscript from *Novy Mir*'s editorial office.

This incident illustrates both the strengths and weaknesses of the democratic fashion in which *Novy Mir* was run. While Tvardovsky was indisputably *primus inter pares* and exerted a cohesive influence over the editorial board, one of his most firmly held beliefs was in the value of collective decision making. This avoided the faults and errors of judgment that can so easily occur in a "one-man band," because Tvardovsky's style was neither "autocratic" nor "hierarchical," as Solzhenitsyn complains in *The Oak and the Calf;* as a matter of principle Tvardovsky sought and acted upon his colleagues' advice—but the line he took might depend on which colleagues happened to have advised him. When reacting spontaneously, Tvardovsky tended to side with the more hawkish policy of the younger members, but if subjected to ideological arguments and pressures he tended to side with his deputies—older and more cautious men. This fluctuation in policy making constituted perhaps as great a threat to the journal's survival as the criticism directed at it from without, for perhaps the most important factor in a journal's policy is the stability and continuity which enables the reader to identify with a definite platform. The younger editors believed that the only way the journal could retain its substantial following among the reading public was by boldly pursuing its goals, as if every issue were the last. They maintained that the cautious approach—of achieving only what was permissible without subjecting the journal to any danger—would be an act of suicide.

In the second part of his article on the relationship between writer, reader, and critic, published in August 1966, Lakshin took the offensive in his self-assigned role of Solzhenitsyn's defense counsel. He said that among readers' letters in response to "Matryona's House" there was not a single negative reaction, proof that the readers perceived the truthfulness of Solzhenitsyn's picture of life and the sincerity of his vision. Unfavorable reactions to the story came from professional critics, whom Lakshin accused of defending the artificial idealization of reality; literature had to be truthful, since if it idealized reality or kept silent about its bad features, it tended to destroy the vital channels of communication between the different parts of a supposedly democratic and socialist society. The paradox of the literary process was that the significance of great works was rarely grasped by society at large; mass psychology tended to be conservative, whereas the role of the artist was progressive—to portray something new and unfamiliar. For this reason the function of the critic was of such crucial importance, for he was required to stand alongside the artist—"among the readers who understand and sympathize with him, and not with the backward section of the public who drag behind the author and hold him back by his coattails." [24] Only by supporting the truth would criticism serve the interests of literature and society.

Under pressure from its conservative watchdogs of culture to take administrative action against *Novy Mir,* at the end of 1966 the Central Committee sacked one of Tvardovsky's deputies, Dement'ev, and the secretary, Zaks, without consulting Tvardovsky. This was a warning to the editorial board to toe the Party line or they too could face dismissal. This form of the insult so incensed Tvardovsky that he almost resigned in protest, as the enemies of *Novy Mir* no doubt hoped. Ironically, however, this action served to strengthen the editorial unity of *Novy Mir,* for Dement'ev and Zaks had been the most conservative members of the board and had continually acted as a brake on Tvardovsky. Their removal weakened the old guard as an effective force within the journal and gave the younger faction greater weight in the policy-making process at *Novy Mir.* Tvardovsky appointed Vinogradov as head of literary criticism, and promoted Lakshin to deputy editor. This so annoyed the Writers' Union bureaucrats that they refused to give Lakshin official recognition.[25] Lakshin had not only threatened their position as writers and critics by his attack on normative criticism; he was also undermining their status as guardians of ideology by encouraging the reading public to form its own value judgments on literature and to draw its own conclusions about how these values should be applied in a social context. By going a long

way toward restoring literary criticism to the com-
manding position it had occupied in the nineteenth-
century thick journal, Lakshin was destroying their
political *raison d'être*. Now they were faced with the fact
of Lakshin holding an even more important office in
Novy Mir, in which he would be able to exert his
influence over every section of the journal.

The sacking of Dement'ev and Zaks thus healed the
split within the journal by abolishing one of its factions. The new unity of the editorial board gave added
strength to its critical platform.

The Political Philosophy of *Novy Mir*

In March 1967 Tvardovsky was summoned to the
Writers' Union Secretariat to account for his journal's
"excessive liberalism." [26] He refused to make a report,
saying that every issue of the journal was tantamount
to a statement of the editorial board's activities. He
did not consider the role of *Novy Mir* as spokesman for
the liberal intelligentsia to be the result of particular
valor on the part of the editorial board, but of a response by the significant sector of public opinion
which supported it. Tvardovsky pointed out the discrepancy between the public's view of *Novy Mir* and
that of the journal's official critics. The latter reacted
as if *Novy Mir*'s line opposed the Party line. But, said
Tvardovsky, "a journal's line is an individual, concrete
expression of the Party's line; it is the journal's physiognomy, defined in the unity of its ideological and
aesthetic preferences and principles." [27] He denied the
accusation made by *Oktyabr'* [28] that *Novy Mir* catered to
those members of the intelligentsia who, were it not
for *Novy Mir*, would send their works to be published
abroad as Sinyavsky had done. Tvardovsky not only

refuted this attack but went further by expressing concern that manuscripts were being locked away while a free press was being formed abroad. He attacked censorship as a relic of the past and called for greater daring in the publication of literature in the Soviet Union.

According to Solzhenitsyn, it was on the day after this meeting that he went to see Tvardovsky and urged him to remove the journal's "voluntary muzzle." Tvardovsky for his part accused Solzhenitsyn of harming the journal by all his public activities, and they quarreled and parted with Solzhenitsyn believing that their cooperation had come to an end. Solzhenitsyn had already chosen the path of political protest; in May 1967 he circulated his open letter to the Fourth Writers' Congress, calling for the complete abolition of censorship. Although Tvardovsky approved of the letter on the grounds that it appealed to Soviet and not Western public opinion, he did not regard Solzhenitsyn's tactics as appropriate to an official Soviet journal like *Novy Mir*. What they had in common was a belief in the necessity for *glasnost'* (openness), but their ultimate aims diverged considerably. By 1967 Solzhenitsyn was seeking to challenge the authority of the Soviet régime, and his actions led logically to an all-out confrontation. *Novy Mir* under Tvardovsky sought to change the system from within, and through cooperation with the Party. Tvardovsky envisaged his journal as moving parallel with Party policy, influencing it, interacting with it, and functioning with a measure of political independence. Solzhenitsyn's principal accusation against *Novy Mir* in his memoir is that it failed to apply an absolute ethical standard to its achievements: the journal published what it *could* publish rather than what it *should have* published. He claims that the journal should have tested the limits of permissibility in every section of every issue. Solzhenitsyn either fails to perceive that such a policy would have been in contradiction with the aims of the editorial board and the political role they envisaged for the journal, or if he did perceive it he refuses to accept it. In his role of dissenter outside the system, Solzhenitsyn is imposing his standards in retrospect on an official Soviet publication which was operating within the system.

The differences between *Novy Mir* and Solzhenitsyn did not lie only in their tactics towards the régime. They also held opposing beliefs on what was desirable for Soviet society, consequently their political goals diverged. The roots of cooperation between the journal and Solzhenitsyn lay in their mutual hatred of Stalinism and the rigid, bureaucratic *dirigisme* which passes for socialism in the USSR. While Khrushchev was in power, the full weight of their criticism was directed against the Stalinist system, a standpoint which had the official blessing of the Twentieth and Twenty-second Party Congresses. After 1965, however, when further criticism of Stalin was banned by the new political leadership, there was a return to the characteristic mentality of the Stalin era which classified any statement as being either for or against Soviet power. *Novy Mir* supported the Revolution and sincerely believed in socialism as an ideal political system. Solzhenitsyn had long since rejected both, although he had kept this well concealed. As Lakshin explains in his essay: ". . . we believed in a socialism that was human through and through and not just with a human face."

Like the other members of *Novy Mir*'s editorial board, Lakshin was prepared to admit the failures of socialism in the Soviet Union, but he attributed these to the persistence of the social influences and traditions of prerevolutionary Russia. Unlike Solzhenitsyn, he believed in socialism as an idea and a principle. This was what so irked Solzhenitsyn about him: Lakshin was a convinced Communist, who joined the Party in 1966. Whereas in Tvardovsky there was a constant inner struggle between his artistic convictions and his sense of obligation to the Party, Lakshin was able to harmonize his political and artistic credo. Moreover, he expressed his beliefs simply and eloquently in his articles in *Novy Mir* and thus, to Solzhenitsyn, was a potential advocate of Marxism-Leninism.

Novy Mir held that the only way in which the failures of Soviet socialism could be rectified was by enlightening and educating the public to a sense of morality. Moral principles, not coercion or blind imitation, should be the only basis of individual and collective responsibility. In his search for moral principles in literature, Lakshin returned to the nineteenth-century tradition of the writer as primarily a critic of society. There he found examples of honesty, of a concern for the spiritual life of the individual, and of responsibility to the *narod* (people), which *Novy Mir* incorporated into its socialist philosophy.

This morality could only develop in the Russian people by a gradual process of enlightenment and self-awareness. This belief of Tvardovsky's *Novy Mir*, that the public had to be "enlightened" before any real social changes could occur, linked the journal with Lunacharsky's *Novy Mir* of the 1920s, and with the traditions of the nineteenth-century thick journal. Theirs was not a task of propagandizing, or foisting alien habits and traditions on to the Russian people, but of making them aware of their own intrinsic value. In this sense the aims of Tvardovsky's journal were sin-

cerely democratic: it strove to appeal to the people as a
whole, and not just to a small section of the liberal-
minded intelligentsia. Lakshin believes that the very
existence of such a Soviet (as opposed to *samizdat*)
journal showed a modest growth of socialist democracy in the Soviet Union.

The invasion of Czechoslovakia by Soviet troops in
August 1968 was a decisive moment for those who
were seeking a development of socialist democracy in
the Soviet Union. It was a test of moral and political
conviction, because to protest against the invasion was
to place oneself squarely in the camp of political opposition to the Soviet régime. *Novy Mir* inwardly opposed
the invasion, and yet outwardly approved it. For Solzhenitsyn this double standard spelled the spiritual
death of the journal, since it compromised its own
principles. It is true that for some of the liberal intelligentsia *Novy Mir*'s compromise undermined its credi-
bility as a spokesman, but for others, the editorial
board included, it was more important than ever for
the journal to continue for as long as it could as a representative of the forces of "socialist democracy" in the
Soviet Union.

The Editorial Practice of *Novy Mir*

In his memoir Solzhenitsyn maintains that even in the
post-Czechoslovakia situation *Novy Mir* continued to
regard itself as the focus of progressive thought in the
Soviet Union. He on the other hand characterizes the
activity of the journal in 1968–9 as "light gymnastics
for the intellect," [29] claiming that discussion of the real
problems of Soviet life were moving away from *Novy
Mir* into *samizdat*. On the other hand, Zhores Medvedev points out that subscriptions to *Novy Mir* contin-

ued to rise in 1969 and that the journal's reception by the liberal intelligentsia was "enthusiastic." He lists a large number of truthful "socially conscious" works which appeared in *Novy Mir* in 1969 by such authors as Fyodor Abramov, Vasil' Bykov, Efim Dorosh, Yury Trifonov, and Georgii Vladimov.[30]

A brief survey of the journal's content for 1969 will indicate whether it was still successful in translating its principles into practice.

Throughout the 1960s the orientation of both fiction and journalism in *Novy Mir* was toward revealing social truths. What unified the different sections of the journal was their shared code of morality, as formulated by Lakshin in his critical articles. From short stories to articles on scientific problems, the fundamental question of values was at the core of every issue.

Thematically, fiction in *Novy Mir* in the 1960s falls under two broad headings, "village prose" and "urban prose." [31] Village prose developed out of the essay of the 1950s, which had been used to present a realistic, documentary-like picture of rural life and to advocate certain economic solutions. Village prose writers of the 1960s moved beyond a narrow economic framework to explore traditional social and cultural patterns of peasant life. *Novy Mir* was mainly representative of the sociopolitical type of village prose, with its aim to reevaluate the historical contribution of the peasantry to Soviet life.[32] It was concerned with peasant values and their role in a now predominantly urbanized society. *Novy Mir,* however, was almost devoid of the nostalgia for a lost way of life that was typical of the neo-Slavophile journal, *Molodaya Gvardiya.*[33]

The writer who best exemplifies the position of *Novy Mir* on rural culture is Vasily Shukshin. His peasant characters are always firmly set in the social background of the village and carry their cultural heritage with them when transplanted to an urban environment. They also embody a spiritual quest for something that transcends the everyday material existence of the village. Shukshin portrays this quest as an intrinsic part of the peasant soul, which is sensitive to depths of emotion and understanding that are inaccessible to the superficial, conformist mentality of the city dweller. The gulf between village and city culture is most clearly manifested in confrontations between the peasantry and the bureaucracy, particularly those who represent the law. In a story called "The Trial," published in *Novy Mir* in 1969,[34] a peasant offers a gift to a judge out of pure gratitude after he has justly won his case. Not until the judge slams the door in his face does he realize that he has behaved wrongly according to the urban bureaucratic ethic.

Other stories by Shukshin, published in *Novy Mir* in 1969, are a chronicle of peasant virtues: honesty, generosity, compassion, respect for the individual, trust in other people. In Solzhenitsyn's Matryona these virtues were embodied in a single moral type, whereas Shukshin highlights different facets of the peasant character in a variety of individuals. His very lack of search for a single hero and total refusal to idealize the peasantry as a social model worthy of nationwide emulation serve to underline more convincingly the central point of Shukshin's stories: the need to preserve the values inherent in a national culture where individual qualities are allowed spontaneous self-expression without bureaucratic interference. The fundamental humanity and morality of this culture is thrown into relief when it is contrasted with the materialism and pseudoculture of the urban neobourgeoisie, as in the story "The Brother-in-Law Sergei Sergeyich."

Urban prose in the 1960s lacked a critical sociological tradition in Soviet literature. Whereas the rural sector had been acknowledged as problematic by the Party since the early 1950s, the correctness of Stalinist methods of industrialization had never been questioned, for obvious ideological reasons. Consequently, urban prose in *Novy Mir* lacked a rationale for reevaluating the industrialized element of Soviet society. It still managed, however, to criticize many aspects of the system of industrial relations and, in particular, to touch on the crucial problem of alienated labor in the Soviet Union. Stories such as Voinovich's "I Want to be Honest" and Solzhenitsyn's "For the Good of the Cause" showed up the discrepancy between moral principles and pragmatic political requirements.

The stream of urban prose in *Novy Mir* culminated in two major works which appeared in the journal in late 1969, Natalya Baranskaya's "A Week Like Any Other" and Yury Trifonov's "The Exchange." Both stories looked at relations within the family in an urban setting. Baranskaya's story shows the hardships of being a Soviet woman, forced to contend with difficult working conditions and the pressures of looking after a home and raising a family. Trifonov focuses on the exchange of a room, but he is less concerned with the practical issue of housing shortages in the Soviet Union than with the moral dilemma underlying it. His hero Dmitriev is accused by his mother of "exchanging himself." The exchange of the room is merely symbolic of the exchange of a whole way of life, with the ideals and values embodied in it.

The values underlying urban prose were essentially the same as those which concerned Shukshin: a rejection of superficial materialism and of political pragmatism. Urban prose took up the moral quest for something to fill the vacuum of contemporary urban life, and sought a spiritual revival within a socialist revival—a return to principles of genuine collectivism, humanism, and democracy. Whereas under Stalin ethics had been subjected to politics in order to justify pragmatic policies, the situation was now reversed and politics were subjected to ethical criteria. This was the essence of *Novy Mir*'s moral stance in the 1960s.

In its economics section for 1969, *Novy Mir* remained firmly committed to the 1965 reforms, despite the fact that these had been abandoned by the Party in the previous year. Its economics spokesman, G. Lisichkin, pleaded the case on moral and economic grounds for a genuinely collective form of organization of agriculture, rather than state ownership and control.[35]

After defining the ethical basis of its socialist platform, the next logical step was for *Novy Mir* to suggest how the participation of the individual in responsible decision making could be guaranteed in practice. The journal did not, however, have a politics section, in the same way that it had an economics or science section, since Soviet politics are considered to be the prerogative of the Party leadership. Hence, as in the nineteenth-century thick journal, political problems had to be discussed indirectly, through literature, philosophy, or history. The only place where politics were called by name in *Novy Mir* was in the headings of the book review section, coupled with science. It was here that in 1969 there appeared an analysis of the prospects of socialist democracy in the Soviet Union. Its author Savin held that this was a qualitatively new and higher stage of democracy, of which the basic features were the participation of all members of society in governing the state, the guarantee of full democratic rights for all citizens, persuasion as the basic method of achieving socialist democracy, and the growing role of social organizations in government. As well as approving a proposal for decentralization, Savin added his own suggestion: that the significance of elections be increased by nominating several candidates. In stressing the principle of genuine electoral choice for the voters, Savin went further than Andrei Sakharov in his 1968 memorandum published in the West under the title "Progress, Coexistence, and Intellectual Freedom."

Thus it can be seen that even in the oppressive political climate that followed the Soviet invasion of Czechoslovakia, *Novy Mir* managed to continue its outspoken criticism and to prove thereby that it was still possible to discuss openly social and political problems in an official Soviet publication.

The Political Role of *Novy Mir*

The fundamental political belief expressed by *Novy Mir* under Tvardovsky was that personal freedom was compatible with communism. Even after the invasion of Czechoslovakia, the journal continued to proclaim the validity of this conviction. Yet this was a direct challenge to the authority of the Communist Party, which substituted "Party-mindedness" for individual conscience. How, in that case, did Tvardovsky's *Novy Mir* manage to survive so long?

There were a number of factors that combined to maintain the existence of *Novy Mir* throughout the 1960s. First, the prestige of Tvardovsky was of enormous importance. The journal was, of course, the product of a collective effort and had an extremely dedicated editorial staff, but it would not have possessed its unique social significance in the 1960s without the leading role of Tvardovsky. He exercised a moral influence over his colleagues that was a crucial binding ingredient in preserving the *esprit de corps* of the journal, even after he ceased to play a prominent part in the everyday affairs of the office from 1966 onward. Lakshin denies that there was a "cult" of Tvardovsky; rather, everyone—friends and foes alike—admired and respected his honesty, courage, and integrity. Tvardovsky was a highly regarded figure in Soviet literature and politics; even when he was eventually ousted in 1970, the Central Committee did not feel able to dismiss him; Tvardovsky had to be manoeuvered into a forced resignation.

A psychological factor in ensuring the survival of *Novy Mir* was the Russian addiction to fanciful rumors as a means of explaining the inexplicable. The fact that it was commonly believed that *Novy Mir* had a highly placed secret benefactor encouraged people to send their works to the journal which they might otherwise have kept to themselves. Another intangible source of strength was the fact that since the editorial board thought that every issue might be the last, they felt they had nothing to lose by adhering to their principles. The more steadfast they were, the more confidence they inspired in the reading public and the harder they were for their opponents to combat.

Of course *Novy Mir* was not able to operate without some patronage from highly placed figures in the Central Committee. Its survival depended in large measure on the support which its political platform enjoyed among the upper ranks of the Party. During the Khrushchev period there was no need to look beyond

the Party leader for the most authoritative patron of
Novy Mir, even if his protection was usually felt only
indirectly. It is well known that it was Khrushchev
himself who championed the publication of Solzhenitsyn's first story and forced its passage through the
Praesidium. When, however, he failed to win a stable
majority for his administrative policies, he was put under increasing pressure by his conservative opponents
to retreat from destalinization. Thus the patronage
afforded to *Novy Mir* by Khrushchev was not a guarantee of the journal's survival; on the contrary, as
Khrushchev's authority gradually diminished, *Novy
Mir,* which was tacitly linked with Khrushchev's
name, also suffered increasing setbacks. When
Khrushchev was eventually removed, Tvardovsky was
relieved, as he felt this allowed him a greater degree of
manoeuvre.

Although the collective leadership which succeeded
Khrushchev allowed for a differentiation of opinion
within the Party, the period from 1965 to 1968 also
marked a gradual shift from destalinization to a limited restalinization. During this transitional period
there was a delicate balance of political forces within
the upper ranks of the Party. *Novy Mir* was able to
maintain its anti-Stalinist position, and even to elabo-
rate a social and economic program. The fact that it
was allowed to continue as a forum for liberal-minded
reformists was a sign that it reflected similar tendencies within the Central Committee. No Party official,
however, openly aligned himself with the political position adopted by *Novy Mir.* Probably no such patron
existed, although it could be conjectured that Kosygin
supported *Novy Mir* since the journal was an ardent advocate of his economic reforms.

During the period 1965 to 1968 the consensus within the Politburo[36] belonged to moderates who opposed Khrushchev's shock methods of destalinization as a dangerous political course but recognized the need for some measure of economic and social reform. While these moderates no doubt held differing opinions of individual issues and would argue them out before formulating official Party policy, they were unified in their opposition to what they regarded as extremist positions, whether they took the form of the neo-Stalinism of *Oktyabr'*, the neo-Slavophilism of *Molodaya Gvardiya,* or the overt anti-Stalinism of *Novy Mir.* According to Viktor Perel'man, who worked on *Literaturnaya Gazeta* in 1968, of these three tendencies *Novy Mir* aroused the greatest hostility in the Central Committee, and people were always asking how much longer it could survive. The fact that it did survive for so long proves either that it enjoyed some support within the Politburo that needed to be reckoned with, or at least no group in the Politburo wished to move decisively against it. For *Novy Mir* played a political role which served the purposes of the Party leadership. This role consisted of preserving a balance of political forces by acting as a counterweight to the neo-Stalinist mouthpiece *Oktyabr';* acting as a sounding board for trying out various reformist ideas, some of which could then be wholly or partly incorporated into official policy; functioning as a safety valve for the liberal-minded intelligentsia who had no other legal forum where they could air their views on current issues. This clearly differed from the role which *Novy Mir* envisaged for itself. It sought to achieve more than play the passive role of a counterweight or safety valve; its positive aim was to enlighten public opinion about what it considered to be the true nature of socialism. At the same time, as a kind of "liberalizing lobby" it sought to convince the Party of the correctness of its program and thereby to swing the balance of political forces in its favor.

The Reasons for the Breakup of the *Novy Mir* Editorial Board and Its Consequences

There seems little doubt that *Novy Mir* did exercise a significant influence on the reading public and to a great extent fulfilled its self-assigned role of enlightener. The journal's impact on Party policy is more difficult to assess but the measures taken against it, such as the designation of a special functionary on *Literaturnaya Gazeta* appointed by the Central Committee to write articles attacking *Novy Mir,* indicated that it was considered a force to be kept in check. Clearly, the ideological alternative it represented was regarded as a potential threat to the status quo. The sense of insecurity promoted by the very existence of *Novy Mir* was increased by the events in Czechoslovakia in 1968, for they showed up the potentially dangerous political role of the liberal intelligentsia and the media. The democratic movement was there in embryo; all it needed was an opportunist like Khrushchev and there could be a new and more dangerous upsurge of destalinization. *Novy Mir* was an important breeding ground of this democratic movement; under Tvardovsky it had become a mouthpiece of the liberal intelligentsia. Many of the writers associated with the journal had signed protests, particularly against the trial of Galanskov and Ginzburg in early 1968; these included Voinovich, Dombrovsky, Iskander, Kaverin, Kopelev, Svetov, and several other critics. There was the potential danger that *Novy Mir* might become an organiza-

tional base for political dissenters. The Soviet leaders
had learned their lesson the hard way: there was a thin line between permissible criticism, which they could patronize for their own benefit, and dissidence, which they could not so easily control.

Hence in the more repressive political climate after the invasion of Czechoslovakia the Party leadership decided to stamp out all signs of heterodoxy. First they moved against individual dissidents whose human-rights activity was based outside the establishment; by the spring of 1969 they had taken firm steps to suppress this manifestation of political independence. Subsequently they turned their attention to the most renowned dissident who was still operating partially within the establishment—Solzhenitsyn—and orchestrated his expulsion from the Writers' Union. At the same time, they initiated a campaign to close down or reconstitute *Novy Mir,* which had fostered Solzhenitsyn and other notable dissidents such as Nekrasov and Voinovich.

In the spring of 1969 *Novy Mir* engaged in an apparently harmless polemic with *Molodaya Gvardiya,* attacking its neo-Slavophilism from an orthodox Marxist-Leninist standpoint.[37] The journal was then accused by eleven conservative writers in a letter to the magazine *Ogonyok* of cultivating a skeptical view of Soviet society and even of representing a "Czechoslovakian deviation." The tone of the letter suggested the start of a large-scale political campaign against *Novy Mir.* The mood of the editorial board was fatalistic as they waited for the final blow. Then *Novy Mir* suffered a double setback: the appearance of Tvardovsky's poem *By Right of Memory* in the émigré journal *Posev* and the expulsion of Solzhenitsyn from the Writers' Union. The conservative leaders of the Writers' Union tried to persuade Tvardovsky to resign for health reasons. When this device failed, they proposed the reorganization of his editorial board but Tvardovsky again refused to cooperate. He decided that if his deputies were removed without his consent he would resign; if not, he would withstand all pressures and remain as editor.

In February 1970 a session was held of the Bureau of the Board of the Writers' Union Secretariat—composed of a small core of conservatives—to reorganize *Novy Mir* without consulting Tvardovsky. The two deputy editors, Lakshin and Kondratovich, were relieved of their posts, as were Vinogradov and Sats. Tvardovsky at once protested to the Central Committee that his editorial board had been reshuffled without the customary procedure of obtaining his consent, but the next day *Literaturnaya Gazeta* carried the announcement that four members of *Novy Mir's* editorial board had been removed; publication of this notice meant that Tvardovsky's appeal had been rejected. Tvardovsky immediately signed a request to be relieved of his post, and was followed by Dorosh, Maryamov, and Khitrov.

The breakup of Tvardovsky's journal had two vital political consequences that were closely interlinked. First, it meant the end of the possibility of legally and openly expressing liberal, reformist ideas in the Soviet Union. The destruction of *Novy Mir* thus stimulated the growth of samizdat in the early 1960s. The second consequence of this act of repression was the final polarization of political positions into "pro-Soviet" and "anti-Soviet," which was a sure sign of restalinization. In the 1960s the political struggle had been between different currents of socialist thought and different tendencies within the Party. *Oktyabr'* had represented the neo-Stalinist position at one end of the spectrum, and *Novy Mir* the anti-Stalinist position at the other. Now that there was no longer a freedom of choice within a socialist framework, the liberal intelligentsia was forced to accept or at least tolerate the official Party line, which had moved closer towards neo-Stalinism, or to reject the Party's authority and move right outside the political establishment. Such a polarization of positions was an inevitable consequence of the abolition of the officially acknowledged, liberal-reformist platform in Soviet politics. This helps explain why many of the writers and critics associated with *Novy Mir* became outspoken dissidents after 1970.

The only medium of free expression—*samizdat*—thus became synonymous with opposition to the Soviet system. Yet many liberal-minded socialists did not regard themselves as in opposition to the system; like Tvardovsky and his editorial board they were seeking an official role of cooperation with the Party leadership in reforming the present system. They did not wish to align themselves with antisocialist forces among the dissidents. This situation was redressed somewhat by the creation in 1975 of a new *samizdat* journal called *Dvadtsaty vek* (*Twentieth Century*) edited by Roy Medvedev and Raissa Lert. However, as an unofficial publication, its influence is limited to a small circle of the intelligentsia. It lacks the legal basis and the large readership which was an essential component of the dual political task of *Novy Mir*: to reflect and to form public opinion in Soviet society as a whole. For *Novy Mir* believed that without an enlightened public opinion and a socialist consciousness, genuine democratization would never take root in the Soviet Union.

The death of Tvardovsky in December 1971 marked the end of a period of optimism, for throughout his editorship the hope had remained that Marxism-Leninism could be combined with freedom of ideas and genuine criticism. Tvardovsky had sincerely believed in this and had attempted to practice it in his journal. At his funeral a woman is reported to have called out: "Is it possible that no one is going to say that we are burying our civic conscience here?" The official press obituary, sighed by the entire Politburo, passed over in silence Tvardovsky's sixteen years of service to *Novy Mir*.

Alexander Solzhenitsyn, Maria Tvardovsky (Alexander
Tvardovsky's widow), and Vladimir Lakshin at Tvardovsky's
funeral, 1971

Notes

Alexander Tvardovsky: A Biographical Study

1. No single English word captures the full meaning of this word which falls somewhere between "people" and "masses."

2. During the period of collectivization, peasants who were relatively well off, who had aroused the envy or dislike of poorer peasants or had somehow offended local officials were labeled *kulaks* and were exiled to Siberia and Northern Russia.

3. From selected correspondence between Tvardovsky and Isakovsky, published in the journal *Druzhba narodov,* No. 8, Moscow, 1976, p. 261.

4. Most of this account of Tvardovsky's spiritual crisis is based on an interview on 14 January 1976 in Moscow. Veiled references to it can also be found in P. S. Vykhodtsev, *Aleksandr Tvardovsky* (Moscow, 1958), pp. 288, 408.

5. David Burg and George Feiffer, *Solzhenitsyn* (New York, 1972), p. 159.

6. V. Pomerantsev, "Ob iskrennosti v literature," *Novy Mir,* No. 12, 1953. A translation of this excerpt can be found in David Burg, "The Cold War on the Literary Front," *Problems of Communism,* September–October 1963, p. 33.

7. Tvardovsky, *Sobranie sochinenii,* III (Moscow, 1966), p. 264.

8. Ibid., p. 273.

9. Interview, 14 January 1976, Moscow.

10. Vladimir Lakshin, "Solzhenitsyn, Tvardovsky and *Novy Mir,"* this volume.

11. This account is based on the story that V. Lakshin told Solzhenitsyn, which the latter relates in *The Oak and the Calf* (hereinafter *The Oak;* New York, 1980), p. 192.

12. Ibid., p. 192.

13. *Literaturnaya Gazeta,* 17 August 1954; article entitled "Za vysokuyu ideinost' nashei literatury."

14. Unfortunately, I have been unable to locate a copy of this

canto. This account is based on verbal information given me by an anonymous but well-informed source on 14 January 1976 in Moscow.

15. Tvardovsky, *Sochineniya* III, p. 207.

16. Ibid., p. 204.

17. Ibid., p. 206.

18. Ibid., p. 216.

19. *Literaturnaya Gazeta,* 24 October 1953, "V redaktsiiu Literaturnoi gazety" (A. Tvardovsky et al.).

20. *Pravda,* 2 February 1959, "Rech' dvadtsat' pervomu s"ezdu KPSS" (A. Tvardovsky).

21. A. Tvardovsky, "Speech to the Third Congress of Writers of the USSR," stenographic report (Moscow, 1959), p. 202.

22. Burg and Feiffer, *Solzhenitsyn,* p. 161. My account of this period is based primarily on the accounts given in this book, Zhores Medvedev's *Ten Years After Ivan Denisovich* (London, 1973), and Solzhenitsyn's *The Oak and the Calf.*

23. *Pravda,* 29 October 1961, "Rech' dvadtsat' vtoromu s"ezdu KPSS" (A. Tvardovsky).

24. The editor-in-chief's authority to publish material was not absolute but was limited by restrictions put on "sensitive" topics. For instance, mention of the existence of prison camps was tabu.

25. Solzhenitsyn, *The Oak,* p. 46.

26. ". . . he did sincerely love me, selflessly yet tyranically: as a sculptor loves the work of his hands. . . ." Solzhenitsyn, *The Oak,* p. 54.

27. Alexander Tvardovsky, *Po pravu pamyati* (extracts), in *Posev,* Frankfurt am Main, October 1969, p. 53.

28. Solzhenitsyn, *The Oak,* p. 49.

30. (A. Tvardovsky), "Za ideinost' i sotsialistichesky realizm", *Novy Mir,* April, 1963, p. 9.

31. Ibid., p. 7.

32. Ibid., p. 4.

33. Central Intelligence Agency Biographical Research File, Washington, D. C., "Aleksandr Tvardovsky." Declassified July 1975, p. 6.

34. It is indeed rather ironic that Adzhubei was called upon to publish the poem since, according to Solzhenitsyn and Medvedev, he and Tvardovsky were professional rivals.

35. There are several slightly differing versions of what happened during the selection process. I have relied on Solzhenitsyn's account, Burg and Feiffer's *Solzhenitsyn*, and on Zhores Medvedev, *Ten Years After Ivan Denisovich*.

36. This term literally means "self-publishing"; it refers to the unofficial circulation of documents, manuscripts, etc., not sanctioned by the government.

37. Sydney Ploss: "Russian Progressives Brought Down" in *Los Angeles Times*, 15 March 1970.

38. Ibid.

39. Medvedev, *Ten Years*, p. 17.

40. Interview, 14 January 1976, Moscow (see n. 14 above).

41. A. Tvardovsky, "Po sluchayu yubileia", *Novy Mir*, January, 1965, p. 4.

42. Ibid., p. 5.

43. Ibid., p. 11.

44. Ibid., p. 8.

45. Solzhenitsyn, *The Oak*, p. 102. According to Solzhenitsyn, Teush, at whose apartment he had hidden his archive, had, without Solzhenitsyn's knowledge, transferred much of the material to Zil'berberg's home because he feared that his own apartment was under surveillance.

46. Burg and Feiffer, *Solzhenitsyn*, p. 222.

47. Solzhenitsyn, *The Oak*, p. 126.

48. Ibid., pp. 127–128.

49. Ibid., p. 139.

50. Vladimir Lakshin, "Writer, Reader, Critic: Second Article," in *Novy Mir*, No. 8, 1966, pp. 216–19.

51. N. Belinkova: "The Victories and Downfall of Tvardovsky," in *Novoe Russkoe Slovo*, New York, 16 January 1972.

52. Solzhenitsyn, *The Oak*, p. 154.

53. *Politichesky dnevnik (Political Diary)*, Amsterdam, 1972, Vol. 1, p. 185.

54. Ibid., p. 187. Tvardovsky specifically mentions Chingiz Aitmatov and B. Mozhayev.

55. Ibid., p. 192.

56. Ibid., pp. 192, 195.

57. As the editor of the most influential literary journal in the country and a member of the Writers' Union Secretariat, Tvardovsky must have expected to be asked to give a speech at the Congress. However, he and other writers that the organizers of the Congress feared might speak out about Solzhenitsyn's letter were denied a forum at the Congress. Burg and Feiffer, *Solzhenitsyn*, p. 248.

58. Solzhenitsyn, *The Oak*, p. 194.

59. Tvardovsky, *Sochineniya*, III, p. 313.

60. Ibid., p. 312.

61. Solzhenitsyn, *The Oak*, p. 473.

62. Ibid., p. 186.

63. Ibid., p. 197.

64. Burg and Feiffer, *Solzhenitsyn*, pp. 265–6.

65. Solzhenitsyn, *The Oak*, p. 200.

66. Leopold Labedz (ed.), *Solzhenitsyn: A Documentary Record* (London, 1972), p. 158.

67. Ibid., p. 160.

68. Ibid., p. 176.

69. Medvedev, *Ten Years*, p. 124.

70. The dissident, according to Solzhenitsyn, was I. Vinogradov. *The Oak*, p. 230.

71. According to Solzhenitsyn, *The Oak*, pp. 242–3. Zhores Medvedev maintains that he had begun it several years earlier. *Ten Years*, p. 121.

72. A. Tvardovsky, *Po pravu pamyati* (extracts), *Posev*, October 1969, p. 54.

73. Ibid., p. 55.

74. A. Tvardovsky, *Sochineniya*, V, p. 499.

75. Solzhenitsyn, *The Oak*, p. 228.

76. Ibid., p. 240.

77. Ibid., p. 225.

78. Medvedev, *Ten Years,* p. 123.

79. *Literaturnaya Gazeta,* 11 February 1970.

80. Medvedev, *Ten Years,* p. 103.

81. *Druzhba narodov,* No. 9, p. 263.

82. See Lakshin, "Solzhenitsyn, Tvardovsky, and *Novy Mir.*"

83. Solzhenitsyn, *The Oak,* p. 274.

84. Ibid., p. 280.

85. Medvedev, *Ten Years,* pp. 129–30.

86. Ibid., p. 128.

87. Solzhenitsyn, *The Oak,* p. 319.

88. D. Pospielovsky, "Tvardovsky—Writer, Editor, Citizen," Radio Liberty Research Paper, 1971, p. 1. Dr Pospielovsky maintains that to be bracketed thus with Kozhevnikov, a "third-rate writer" and editor of the conservative journal *Znamya (The Banner)* since 1949, was a calculated insult to Tvardovsky. Perhaps that is the way it appears, but I doubt if the authorities had any real need or desire to injure a very popular poet, who, in any case, lay on his deathbed.

89. Medvedev, *Ten Years,* pp. 166–7. The translation by Michael Scammell appeared in the London newspaper *The Observer,* 9 January 1972. The complete text can be found in Solzhenitsyn, *The Oak,* p. 274.

90. Lakshin, "Solzhenitsyn, Tvardovsky and *Novy Mir.*"

91. Solzhenitsyn, *The Oak,* p. 31.

92. Interview, 14 January 1976, Moscow (see n. 14 above).

The Politics of *Novy Mir* under Tvardovsky

1. No. 9, 1927

2. A theory propagated by the Left Futurists in the journal *Novy LEF* (1927–8; a successor to *LEF*), according to which a work of art must fill a particular social need of the dominant class (i.e., the working class) and that such needs could only be interpreted by

artists and writers who were truly in touch with the aspirations of the class.

3. No. 1, 1965.

4. *Bolshevik,* No. 19–20, 1931.

5. There are exceptions, such as the closure of *Leningrad* in 1946.

6. "Raionnye budni," in *Novy Mir,* No. 9, 1952, and No. 3, 1954.

7. V. Lakshin, "Writer, Reader, Critic," *Novy Mir,* No. 4, 1965.

8. From a private interview with Lakshin.

9. L. Gruliow and C. Saikovski (eds.) *Current Soviet Policies—IV: The Documentary Record of the XXII Congress of the CPSU* (New York, 1962), p. 189.

10. A. Solzhenitsyn, *The Oak and the Calf,* p. 33.

11. This literally means "self-flowing." It denotes the inflow of unsolicited material into editorial offices.

12. The most active members of any group.

13. Tvardovsky's definition in "On the Occasion of the Anniversary," *Novy Mir,* No. 1, 1965.

14. "Ivan Denisovich, His Friends and Foes," *Novy Mir,* No. 1, 1964.

15. Ibid., p. 226.

16. Ibid., p. 233.

17. No. 2, 1964.

18. Nos. 7 and 8, 1964.

19. No. 1, 1965.

20. Ibid., p. 14.

21. Dement'ev was a deputy editor and Zaks was the board's secretary, Kondratovich was also deputy editor but appears to have been more of a neutral figure.

22. From a private interview with Lakshin.

23. *The Oak,* p. 133. This is Solzhenitsyn's account of events but the basic information has been corroborated by Vinogradov.

24. *Novy Mir,* No. 8, 1966, p. 255.

25. He was not credited as deputy editor in the back of *Novy Mir,* whose status is that of an organ of the Writers' Union.

26. *Politichesky dnevnik (Political Diary)*, Amsterdam, 1972, vol. 1, p. 184.

27. Ibid., p. 185.

28. *Oktyabr' (October)*, edited by Kochetov, was the leading conservative journal.

29. *The Oak,* p. 244.

30. Zh. Medvedev, *Ten Years After Ivan Denisovich* (London, 1973), p. 121.

31. "Village prose" is an accepted literary description; "urban prose" is my own term.

32. Such writers as Abramov, Zalygin, and Mozhayev.

33. "Neo-Slavophilism" is a recent literary trend in the USSR, associated with the journals *Molodaya Gvardiya (Young Guard)* and *Ogonyok (The Flame)*, chiefly during the period 1965–9, but to some extent persisting to the present day. It is characterized by an approving attitude to the Stalinist past and a nostalgic fondness for native Russian culture. The movement also contains certain elements of Russian nationalism and anti-semitism. The political aspects of "neo-Slavophilism" were also to be found in the journal *Oktyabr'* under the editorship of Vsevolod Kochetov (d. 1977).

34. No. 10, 1969.

35. "Man—Cooperation—Society," No. 5, 1969.

36. In 1966 the Praesidium was renamed the Politburo.

37. A. Dement'ev, "On Traditions and Nationalism," No. 4, 1969.